The Backpacker's Guide to the
LAKE DISTRICT

The Backpacker's Guide to the
LAKE DISTRICT
The 40 Best Two-Day Fell Walks

Graham Thompson

DAVID & CHARLES

Sharp Edge, Blencathra

DEDICATION

For Dawn, whose continual support made it possible to complete this book, and for Nima our four-legged companion who never tires of walking the fells.

DISCLAIMER

Please remember that the mountains can be very dangerous places and are ventured onto at your own risk. Walkers must use their own judgement and assess local conditions before venturing onto the hills. This book is not an instructional manual and neither the author nor the publishers can accept any responsibility for any accident, injury, loss or damage sustained while following any of the routes described.

Page 1: A lone tree in Ennerdale
Page 2–3: View over Derwent Water to Cat Bells, Causey Pike and Grisedale Pike

All photographs by Graham Thompson Photo Library
Maps by Graham Thompson and Jeremy Ashcroft

A DAVID & CHARLES BOOK

First published in the UK in 1999

Book design by Les Dominey Design Company
and printed in Hong Kong by Imago
for David & Charles
Brunel House   Newton Abbot   Devon

CONTENTS

INTRODUCTION   6

CIRCULAR ROUTES
NORTHERN FELLS
Route 1:   Keswick to High Row   14
Route 2:   Caldbeck to Cockermouth   17

NORTH-WESTERN FELLS
Route 3:   Buttermere Skyline   19
Route 4:   A Circuit of Crummock
             Water and Loweswater   24
Route 5:   Keswick to Buttermere   27
Route 6:   Cockermouth to Buttermere   32
Route 7:   Bassenthwaite Lake Skyline   35

WESTERN FELLS
Route 8:   Wasdale Skyline   38
Route 9:   Eskdale to Wasdale   42
Route 10: Ennerdale Horseshoe   45
Route 11: Wasdale to Ennerdale   48
Route 12: A Round of Eskdale   51
Route 13: Broughton in Furness
             to Eskdale   54
Route 14: Borrowdale to Wasdale   57
Route 15: Borrowdale to Eskdale   62

CENTRAL FELLS
Route 16: Lakeland's 3000ft Mountains   65
Route 17: Thirlmere Skyline   68
Route 18: Langdale to Eskdale   73
Route 19: Coniston to Langdale   76
Route 20: Coniston to Eskdale   80
Route 21: Derwent Water Skyline   85
Route 22: Langdale Skyline   88

EASTERN FELLS
Route 23: Grasmere to Ullswater   91
Route 24: High Street and Helvellyn
            from Ambleside   95
Route 25: Patterdale to Shap   98
Route 26: Staveley to Shap   101
Route 27: Haweswater Skyline   104
Route 28: Ullswater Skyline   107
Route 29: Threlkeld to Glenridding   112

SOUTHERN FELLS
Route 30: Kendal to Newby Bridge   115
Route 31: A Round of Windermere   118
Route 32: Circuit of Coniston Water   121
Route 33: Newby Bridge to Hawkshead   124
Route 34: Broughton in Furness to
            Coniston   127
Route 35: Spark Bridge to Hawkshead   131

POINT-TO-POINT ROUTES
Route 36: Penrith to Ravenglass via
            Ambleside   134
Route 37: Windermere to Penrith
            via Shap   138
Route 38: Shap to Ravenglass
            via Grasmere   142
Route 39: Silecroft to Borrowdale
            via Eskdale   147
Route 40: Coniston to Keswick
            via Wasdale   151

Getting About   156
Acknowledgements   156
Bibliography   157
Index   158

INTRODUCTION

The Lake District is one of the most popular areas of the British Isles. Its landscape of lakes, rivers, woods, mountains, dales and farms is legendary and has attracted visitors, travellers, explorers, mountaineers, writers and poets for centuries. The Lake District National Park extends for more than 2243sq km and is the largest park of its kind in Britain. It contains the highest mountain in England – Scafell Pike, the deepest lake – Wast Water and the longest lake – Windermere. For the mountain walker there is, arguably, no finer place in England.

The great appeal of the Lake District is its ease of access, making it a focal point for walkers, lovers of mountain scenery and travellers from all around the world. Compared to the Himalayas, the Alps, or even the Scottish Highlands, the fells of the Lake District are moderate in size and the area of the National Park is small in comparison to their greater ranges but it is this size that is part of the attraction, as a walker can climb a mountain and return to base within a day. The size of the Lake District also means that walkers can experience a two-day walk across the mountains and still stay in close proximity to their home comforts. For example, you can walk all the way across the Lake District National Park in just two days, without the need to carry tents or food. There are also many friendly inns, hotels and bed and breakfast establishments along the way where you can put your feet up beside a log fire and enjoy friendly hospitality, good beer and tasty food. Alternatively you could spend the night in a tent in an isolated mountain campsite, youth hostel, bothy or camping barn – there is a type of accommodation to suit everyone's idea of comfort, fun and adventure.

It is this aspect of walking in the Lake District that makes this book so different and unique, for here is a collection of walks that take the visitor on a series of two-day adventures that will fit neatly into their weekend break. The book is designed to be a reference guide to the walking opportunities of the Lake District. The routes cover most corners of the National Park and aim to travel over the fells whenever possible. Some routes are intentionally designed to follow valleys and many of these trace the passage of Roman legions, drovers and traders that have crossed these mountains for centuries.

Using This Guide

For the purpose of this book the Lake District National Park has been divided into six regions: the Northern Fells, North-western Fells, Western Fells, Southern Fells, Eastern Fells and Central Fells. Anyone who knows the Lake District will realise that I have not included a separate Far Eastern Fells group, but fear not, these have been included in the Eastern Fells section as too many of the routes overlapped into both areas to make the division workable. Apart from the circular routes divided into these sections, there is also a seventh group of point-to-point routes which make crossings of the Lake District from most directions using accommodation in the heart of the country half-way through the journey.

The book has been designed as a work of reference and inspiration. The descriptions and maps are provided as a general guide to the area so that you may select a route and prepare your weekend away. The descriptions outline the route to be followed and highlight points of interest along the way. The colour photographs have been chosen to capture a little of the magic of Lakeland as well as to reveal the topography of the routes.

The walks have been chosen for their character, quality and practicability, combined with their access to accommodation and public transport. The routes range from established classic challenge events to walks that cross virtually untracked terrain where very few people have walked to this day. There are, however, more routes available in the Lake District than can fit into any book and those included here are what I regard to be the best cross-section of what is available. Therefore I encourage readers to modify these routes to suit their own personal desires as almost every route has a wide and fascinating variety of alternative paths.

Route Names

For ease of reference, each route is given the name of the area over which it travels. On the circular routes this means they are named after the start point and half-way point – this being the extreme ends of the area travelled in one direction before returning to the start. On point-to-point routes, the start and finish points are used in the route name. In some cases where the walk is based around a traverse of a feature, such as a valley or lake, this is used in the title, for example, the Buttermere Skyline.

Circular Walks

There are thirty-five circular walks within six sections, but as many routes are long they naturally stray into neighbouring regions. These walks all start and finish at the same point and are based around accommodation such as a campsite, youth hostel, hotel or B&B at the end of each day.

Point-to-Point Routes

There are five routes that travel across the Lake District National Park from one point to another. These start and finish at different places and make use of accommodation such as a campsite, youth hostel, hotel or B&B at the end of each day. To make these routes as easy to organise as possible, they are all based around public transport services, with regular connections to the original start point or to the main line railway services.

Distance

All the walks take a logical route over the fell tops or valleys. This means that routes vary in length but most can easily be achieved over a two-day period while a couple of the routes are recognised as classic challenges that require a high level of fitness to be completed within the two days. In particular Route 16 Lakeland's 3000ft Mountains and Route 36 Penrith to Ravenglass via Ambleside are very long indeed. To complete these walks over two days you will need to travel with a very light rucksack and be fitter than average. There are, however, a number of routes that are quite short and can easily be completed over a two-day period and some, such as Route 3 Buttermere Skyline can be completed by fit walkers in a single day.

Total Ascent

All the routes give a guide to the amount of ascent and re-ascent covered during each day of walking. It follows that a short walk with a high level of ascent will be harder that a short walk with little ascent,

therefore the hardest and most challenging routes are those that include a long distance as well as a large amount of ascent.

Time

An estimation of the time required to complete each day's walk is provided. This is based on a walking speed of 4km/hour plus thirty minutes for every 300m of ascent, and it allows approximately one hour for rest breaks. This is only an estimate and some walkers may complete the walks faster or slower than this depending on their fitness and whether they are carrying a full load of camping equipment.

Difficulty

A short description of the difficulty of each route has been provided and this includes an overview of the terrain covered as well as a comment on the overall difficulty in terms of navigation, ascent and length.

Accommodation

A short list of where accommodation can be found is provided and where there is little choice it is mentioned here. A wide choice of accommodation is available in the Lake District but things change from year to year, so it is always best to check with the tourist information centres when planning your trip.

Above: High Stile Ridge from Fleetwith Pike. Buttermere is on the right

Opposite: Off path! Hiker on the crags of Pillar – Ennerdale is the valley beyond

Public Transport

An overview of the available bus and rail services is provided to aid planning. Bus services in the Lake District change from year to year, so it is always best to check with the tourist information centres when planning your trip.

Maps

The Lake District is well mapped by both the Ordnance Survey and Harvey's Walkers Maps. Many of the routes cover two maps although some can be completed with just a single map. The recommended maps are as follows:

Ordnance Survey Landranger (1:50,000)
    89, 90, 96, 97
Ordnance Survey Outdoor Leisure (1:25,000)
    4, 5, 6, 7
Harvey's Walker (1:40,000) and Superwalker (1:25,000) Northwest Lakeland, Western Lakeland, Eastern Lakeland, Southern Lakeland, Central Lakeland.

Photographs

Colour photographs are used throughout the book to
give an impression of the walks and the terrain they
cover. Many of the photographs were taken
specifically for this book and show the fells in their
most splendid light, the finest weather and from the
most picturesque angles. However, it has to be said
that these conditions are often the exception rather
than the rule.

Weather

Although the pictures in this book may imply that the
mountains often bask under fine weather, it must be
stated that they also attract very poor weather. This
can make even the easiest walk very challenging and
sometimes dangerous, therefore all the descriptions in
this book are based on fine weather. All walks on the
Lakeland fells become far more difficult in winter
when snow makes travel more hazardous, so no one
should follow the routes described when the weather
is unfavourable or when snow is on the ground, unless
they are very experienced, trained and correctly
equipped to do so.

Before setting out on any walk in the Lake
District, please consult the local weather forecast and
adjust your plans to suit the prevailing weather
conditions and your ability. Weather bulletins are
updated twice a day by the National Park Authority
based on information from the Meteorological Office.
This is available twenty-four hours a day by
telephoning 017687 75757. Weather bulletins are also
posted at various outdoor shops, youth hostels, hotels
and other sites.

Rights-of-Way

Every care has been taken in the preparation of this
book and the author encountered no difficulty of
access on any of the routes described. However, the
inclusion of a route in this book does not imply that a
right-of-way exists. Please remember that all upland
areas are owned by someone and we walkers are not
free to roam anywhere we wish. Therefore readers are
advised that changes in rights-of-way may occur and
these may affect the routes described. If in doubt
please consult the Definitive Maps held by the Lake

District National Park offices, or seek the landowners'
permission.

Mountain Safety

It is assumed that everyone using this book will have
some mountain walking experience and be familiar
with the equipment and the safety, navigational and
survival techniques required to walk safely in the
mountains.

For those new to mountain walking it is
recommended that they either take a basic course,
join a club, or enlist the assistance of experienced
friends. The potential for accidents is always present,
so it is important that you are prepared for them. To
deal with accidents on the hill, walkers must carry
basic survival equipment and a first aid kit. Apart from
normal walking clothing and equipment, walkers
should carry:

- Map of relevant area
- Compass
- First aid kit
- Survival bag – 2.4 x 1.2m (8 x 4ft) 500-gauge
  polythene bag
- Emergency rations
- Whistle
- Torch

*The International Alpine Distress Signal is six
whistle blasts or flashes of a light followed by a
pause of one minute before repeating. The reply is
three blasts of a whistle or flashes of a light.*

To help the rescue services find you in case of an
accident you should leave the following information
with a responsible person before setting off:

- Name and address
- Time of departure and expected arrival
- Planned route with grid references and
  directions
- Any possible variations that may be taken on
  the route
- Possible escape routes
- Details of medical conditions/problems

The Environment

The Lake District National Park is a beautiful area of mountainous landscape and it is the responsibility of the visitor to ensure that it remains so. Unlike some other parts of the world it is *not* owned by the state and set aside for recreational use: it is privately owned and supports a local working community. So when embarking on a walk through the mountains, we must all be very conscious of the environment and the effect of our actions and activities within it. We should attempt to leave stones unturned and vegetation undisturbed. We should take our waste home and move carefully over the landscape without disturbing breeding birds or tearing up the paths by cutting across the corners of zigzags. The famous Sierra Club motto, 'take only photographs, leave only footprints', is one to keep in mind at all times.

A major problem in the Lake District is the number of cars that block roads and cause pollution. Virtually every walk in this book can be accessed with public transport so there is no need to take the car.

Walkers with dogs must take care throughout the year but particularly during the lambing season from February to May. Even well-behaved dogs can cause sheep great distress when running on the fells. Therefore dogs should be kept on a lead or under close control on the fells at all times.

KESWICK TO HIGH ROW

The natural wilderness that lies 'back o' Skidda' provides a unique opportunity in the Lake District to experience rolling moors with extensive views. Here the walker can undertake long walks, with few crags and few easily recognisable features. This walk makes a two-day traverse of Skiddaw, Blencathra and the highest fells that lie 'back o' Skidda'. It links Lakeland's northern capital, Keswick with the remote backwater around the River Caldew, where Carrock Fell Youth Hostel is ideally placed at High Row for overnight accommodation.

WALK FACTS

Start/Finish	Keswick, GR 268235
Distance	Day one: 24km (15 miles)
	Day two: 22.5km (14 miles)
Total ascent	Day one: 1500m (4922ft)
	Day two: 1100m (3609ft)
Time	Day one: 9 hours
	Day two: 8 hours

Difficulty High-level fell walk over some unpathed featureless rolling moorland where navigation can be very difficult in mist. Optional grade one scramble over Sharp Edge, but this can be avoided easily

Accommodation Campsites, B&Bs and youth hostels at Keswick, High Row (Carrock Fell Youth Hostel) and the surrounding area

Public transport Keswick is well served by bus services which link it with a railway station at Penrith

DAY ONE

The day begins from Keswick, the historical start for a walk up Skiddaw, with people clambering up the mountain since Victorian times. From Keswick walk down Station Road and follow the road sharply right and under the disused railway line to Briar Rigg. Here you must take a bridleway on the right that leads around the lower slopes of Latrigg to the car park on its north side. You can then make a diversion to climb Latrigg, with views from the top extending over Keswick to the Central Fells.

A track leading south-east from Latrigg car park descends to the banks of the Glenderaterra Beck, which is crossed via a footbridge and then you climb to the Blencathra Centre, an outdoor pursuits centre. Now a steep pull awaits you north-east over Blease Fell to Knowe Crags, with ever-expanding views over Keswick and Derwent Water and the mighty Central Fells.

A clear ridge path leads to the summit of Blencathra, with steep cliffs to your right, while in all other directions the slopes are grass covered, smooth and rolling. Leave the summit by heading north around the head of Sharp Edge and Foule Crags to a col at the head of the River Glenderamarkin. More experienced walkers could head for the alternative route over Sharp Edge to the north-west – this arcs around the northern shore of Scales Tarn and provides an airy grade one scramble, though it can be dangerous in the wet, high winds or snow. From the base of Sharp Edge you can turn north and walk up the valley to the col to join the main route.

A stiff climb over a heather fellside leads from the col at the head of the River Glenderamarkin to Bannerdale Crags and then you turn north over Bowscale Fell to Tarn Crags, with tiny Bowscale Tarn resting in its craggy cradle. A long descent north-west takes you over rough heather to cross the unbridged River Caldew. It's then a steep climb north-east to reach Carrock Fell, with its fine views to the Pennines, Skiddaw and Blencathra.

The final part of the walk takes you east from Carrock Fell so that you may descend to Mosedale on a winding trail. Here a variety of accommodation awaits, with a youth hostel at High Row a short walk away along the lane.

ALONG THE WAY

The path that traces the banks of
Carrock Beck towards **High Pike** was
built to serve the mines under High Pike
back in the sixteenth century.
The mines produced a wide variety of
minerals and some yielded as many as
twenty-three different varieties at a time,
but today they all lie dormant.
Great Calva's summit is marked by
a cairn and a fine view, which
leads the eye along a
geographical fault line through
the Glenderaterra valley, down
St John's In the Vale, across
Thirlmere and over Dunmail
Raise to Windermere. The
famous Lakeland guidebook
writer, Alfred Wainwright,
described this as being like
'looking along the sights of a gun'.
Sharp Edge is one of the finest rocky
ridges in the Lake District and England.
It requires the use of hands to negotiate
its narrow ridge, which is short-lived but
testing to the backpacker who is
normally used to walking rather than
scrambling. Sharp Edge is more difficult
and airy than Striding Edge on Helvellyn
and is the only rocky ridge in the
Northern Fells of the Lake District.
Skiddaw is the Lake District's fourth
highest fell at 931m (3054ft) above sea-
level and is also the oldest fell of the
region. Its crumbling slate was standing
proud of the surroundings over 500
million years ago, while the volcanic
rock that formed many of the central
fells didn't exist on the earth's surface.

*View south-west from Carrock Fell
with Skiddaw on the right,
Blencathra on the left*

DAY TWO

The second half of the walk makes a high-level traverse through the heart of the area known as 'back o' Skidda'. But it begins with a valley walk along the banks of Carrock Beck towards High Pike. A series of zigzags lifts you out of the valley and onto the summit, which provides views to the fringe of the Lake District to the west, north and east, while Skiddaw and Blencathra dominate the view to the south.

Walk south-west from High Pike, following the clear Cumbria Way path past Lingy Hut, a popular bivvy site for walkers which is maintained by the Lake District National Park. You round Great Lingy Fell, descend across the soggy head of Grainsgill Beck and then climb to Coomb Height, which projects out on a limb. Your next objective is nearby Knott, which at 710m (2329ft) is the highest point in these fells. This is a truly wild place, with just a simple cairn and virtually no paths.

Leave Knott in a south-westerly direction to find

View east from summit of Doddick Fell, Blencathra

a col that rises between Wiley Gill and Hause Gill. Even in these rolling fells, a long descent means a long ascent, and this comes in the form of a pull south and then south-east to the summit of Great Calva, which is marked with a cairn and has a fine view.

An old fence line leads you north-west and then south-west to Little Calva, before descending west to Whitewater Dash waterfalls, which are the only falls in the area and a popular spot for picnics. Stick with the fence line as it climbs south-west up steep slopes to Bakestall and finally onto Skiddaw's back. From the summit you'll have a greater appreciation of the view, as many of the hills that you can see to the north you will have climbed on your journey. You will also be able to appreciate why the fell is so popular and has been so since Victorian times. A clear path of descent leads south-east from the summit of Skiddaw back to the car park on the edge of Latrigg. You may now retrace your steps back to Keswick.

CALDBECK TO COCKERMOUTH

Skiddaw from the slopes of Binsey

The far north-western corner of the Lake District may not have many high fells but it provides mile after mile of low-level walking potential through country fields and along quiet lanes. Here you can escape from the busy tourist centres and see a part of real Lakeland life as it is today. The walk links Cockermouth and Caldbeck, a town and village on the fringe of the Lake District. They are separated by the lower slopes of Skiddaw and the Northern Fells. Rivers wind between fields of sheep and cattle before diving into woodland. Country lanes link quiet clusters of cottages and remote farms. On the horizon to the south and west are the high fells, while to the north and east the view extends to the Cumbria Coast, the Solway Firth and southern Scotland.

WALK FACTS

Start/Finish	Caldbeck, GR 320400
Distance	Day one: 30.5km (19 miles)
	Day two: 25.7km (16 miles)
Total ascent	Day one: 350m (1148ft)
	Day two: 350m (1148ft)
Time	Day one: 9 hours
	Day two: 8 hours

Difficulty A long, low-level walk on paths and country lanes with very little hill climbing. The walk can be divided in two at Bassenthwaite

Accommodation Campsites, youth hostels, hotels and B&Bs in Cockermouth, Bassenthwaite and Caldbeck

Public transport Cockermouth, Bassenthwaite and Caldbeck are all served by public bus services from Keswick and Penrith railway station

DAY ONE

It's a long walk to Cockermouth but at least it's reasonably flat. However, it's still worth making an early start to avoid a long hike in the dark. You leave Caldbeck on the Cumbria Way and this takes you south towards Nether Row on a quiet lane. Picking your way between footpaths and tracks you rejoin the road at Fellside Farm. But like all the roads in this part of the Lake District, it is quiet and really only serves to link the remote cottages and farms that are scattered along the lower slopes of the Caldbeck and Uldale Fells.

The road becomes a rough track from Greenhead and climbs a little to give views over the farmland around Uldale. The track emerges onto the road once again at Longlands, with a fine view to Over Water, which is popular with local fishermen. The road is followed downhill and then up around Castle How to Orthwaite. Field paths lead the way now, but they are all well signposted. Some care is needed though to find a path to Bassenthwaite, as you must leave the Cumbria Way in the field just before Peter House Farm. Signs do mark the path junction but it's easily missed so keep an eye on your map.

Bassenthwaite is a quiet village with a green, a pub and a church. You could even end the day here and stay in one of the B&Bs or campsites in the area, which would leave you to return to Caldbeck via Binsey on day two. To continue on to Cockermouth, a little road walking is needed to escape from Bassenthwaite. You have to cross the busy A591 and follow the road signs for the B5291 for half a mile before you can turn off onto the Allerdale Ramble. This long-distance path follows the River Derwent to Cockermouth making the second half of the walk very easy on navigation leaving you plenty of time to enjoy the wide vistas over the rolling countryside here at the very edge of the Lake District National Park.

DAY TWO

You have now left the Lake District National Park, as the boundary bypasses the town of Cockermouth. There has often been talk of moving the boundary, but at present this has not been achieved. However, Cockermouth is still a fine, attractive market town, with a wide, tree-lined main street and a number of beautiful Georgian houses. But Cockermouth's most notable claim to fame is as the birthplace of the poet William Wordsworth in 1770. His former home is owned by the National Trust and is open to the public.

The River Cocker cuts through the centre of Cockermouth and joins the River Derwent. The A594 can be followed over the River Derwent and out of town to the north. You can then rejoin the Allerdale Ramble long-distance path, which leads back towards Bassenthwaite. But this time the path makes a northerly arc around Cockermouth to Isle Gate and rejoins the path used on the outward journey during day one. Retrace your steps along the banks of the

River Derwent, past Buckholme Island and around the head of Bassenthwaite Lake to the A591 road.

You leave the Allerdale Ramble once again and head for Binsey, a conical hill rising to the north which provides almost the only uphill struggle of the walk. Link up country lanes and field paths through High Dewaldeth to Fell End Farm at the base of Binsey. A bridleway leads through the fields and onto the summit, where your climb is greeted with a fine view back to Skiddaw and Bassenthwaite Lake.

The bridleway leads from Binsey, north-west to the site of a Roman fort, which would have formed part of the northern guard of the Roman empire along with Hadrian's Wall further to the east of Carlisle. Bridleways and quiet lanes carry you east to High Houses, High Ireby, Ruthwaite and Aughertree. You are now on the boundary of the Lake District National Park and a footpath carries you along the boundary line and around the base of Green How to a minor road. A road walk into Caldbeck is all that remains but like everywhere on this walk there are very few cars to spoil the solitude of this far north-western corner of the Lake District.

ALONG THE WAY

Caldbeck is an attractive village with a green and a duck pond. It's closely associated with the mining industry, which has existed on the Caldbeck Fells since the thirteenth century with lead, copper, wolfram and barytes profitably extracted until the 1960s when the last mine was closed. Caldbeck is perhaps best known though as the resting place of John Peel, the master of a pack of hounds for over fifty years. His claim to fame depends solely on a song , 'Do ye ken John Peel', the words of which were written by a friend to a local tune.
Cockermouth, lying just outside the Lake District National Park boundary, is one of Cumbria's most historic towns with settlements existing in the area since the Iron Age. The Romans built a fort here in the second century AD, which stood at the junction of the Roman roads which extended to Maryport, Penrith and Carlisle.

Another castle was built at Cockermouth in the thirteenth century and it has been owned by

various people over the years. It is now the private residence of Lord Egremont. Cockermouth, like Caldbeck, was home to slate quarrying, along with lead and iron mining. To carry the workers and the ore from the mines, the Cockermouth, Keswick and Penrith Railway Company was provided in 1861 and remained in use up until 1966, when many railway branch-lines throughout Britain were closed to save money.

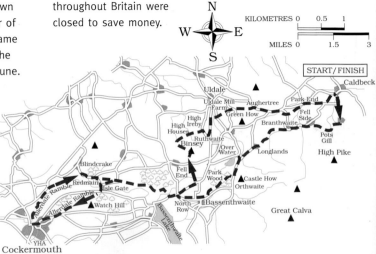

BUTTERMERE SKYLINE

Buttermere can appear as a deep dark hole in stormy weather, when the rain clouds hide its true form. But given a fine spell it can be one of the prettiest places in the Lake District, with lofty ridges and hanging valleys looking down onto its cluster of houses that overlook its lake set in pasture and woodland. The Buttermere horseshoe is a classic Lakeland walk that many walkers could complete in a single long day in summer, but it also fits neatly into a two-day expedition at any time of the year. This more gentle approach to the route allows more time to take in stunning views down the length of Buttermere, which must surely rank among the finest in the Lake District.

WALK FACTS

Start/Finish	Buttermere, GR 174170
Distance	Day one: 9.6km (6 miles)
	Day two: 16km (10 miles)
Total ascent	Day one: 900m (2953ft)
	Day two: 900m (2953ft)
Time	Day one: 5 hours
	Day two: 6 hours

Difficulty A relatively short walk on clear paths over high mountain ridges

Accommodation Youth hostels at Buttermere and Honister Pass, B&Bs and campsites are also available at Buttermere

Public transport Very infrequent bus services link Buttermere with Keswick, from where connections can be made to the railway station at Penrith

DAY ONE

There's a steep climb when you begin any fell walk from Buttermere village and on this route the hard work leads to the summit of Robinson. But with the views growing with every step and the prospect of easier walking ahead, the climb is soon over. Your efforts are rewarded with a scene of shapely fells in every direction, so many that you could stand and gaze for hours without getting bored. Red Pike and the High Stile Ridge look particularly impressive across Buttermere valley and you'll be climbing these fine peaks during day two. The name Robinson comes from Richard Robinson, who purchased a number of estates including the then unnamed fell of Robinson. Originally it was known as Robinson Fell, but today it is simply known as Robinson.

The hard work is now over for the day and all you need do is turn your back on the view and follow the ridge. You begin by heading south to the Littledale Edge, where more spectacular views across Buttermere draw your attention from the leg-work. The ridge maintains its altitude and swings around to the Hindscarth ridge. You should have plenty of time in hand, so a short excursion to the summit of Hindscarth (Old Norse for 'pass of the red deer') should be possible. This is also a great location for a lunch break as you take in the view across the Newlands valley to distant Skiddaw.

Returning to the main ridge you walk easily once more south-east to Dale Head, where a huge cairn marks the summit. Here there is a classic view down the length of the Newlands valley to Skiddaw, with the lakes of Bassenthwaite and Derwent Water adding a seam of sparkling silver to the mountainous scene. Your bed for the night is near as you only need to turn your back on the scene and follow the fence line down to Honister Pass. The old mine workings provide plenty of interest around here and the youth hostel stands on the site of the old mine manager's office.

If you are still feeling fit, you could take a short walk up to Fleetwith Pike to see the sunset. To do so you must follow the old quarry road up from the top of Honister Pass, which is signposted for Great Gable and Dubs Quarry. The track zigzags up to an old winch wheel that was originally installed to help move

View from Honister Crag

slate from the mines. An unclear path leads across the fell becoming clearer as the summit of Fleetwith Pike is reached. On a clear night a spectacular sunset forms that is reflected in the waters of Crummock Water and Buttermere.

DAY TWO

Day two tackles the bounding south rim of Buttermere and once again stunning views are the order of the day. You begin by taking the Great Gable and Dubs Quarry path from behind Honister Youth Hostel which leads onto the old tramway that was originally built to serve the slate mines.

The path descends clearly through the mines to Dubs Bottom, a soggy hollow that has to be crossed before you can climb underneath Green Crag. Enjoyable rambling continues past the still waters of Blackbeck Tarn and then you finally climb to Innominate Tarn. The rocky ground underfoot holds the ashes of the late Alfred Wainwright and many people wanted to rename the tarn as Wainwright

Tarn, but his widow resisted the gesture. Wainwright loved the place because of the views and these are as stunning today as they have always been.

You descend steeply now to cross Scarth Gap Pass, which provides a link between Ennerdale and Buttermere and where iron posts mark the parish boundary of Buttermere. A steep scree slope has to be conquered to reach High Crag. It is a far from pleasant climb but with views to Pillar to the south there is plenty to take your mind off the task. Once the summit is gained the views from High Crag are as fine as any, with the valleys of Ennerdale and Buttermere sweeping up from the south and north.

Easy rambling continues along the High Stile Ridge to Red Pike, the red granite rock of which is clearly visible underfoot. A direct descent can be made to the valley by way of Bleaberry Tarn, but a far superior end to the day is to walk north-west around Ling Comb and down to Scale Beck, where Scale Force cascades through a narrow rocky defile in spectacular fashion. Clear paths lead out of the valley towards Crummock Water and easily back to Buttermere village.

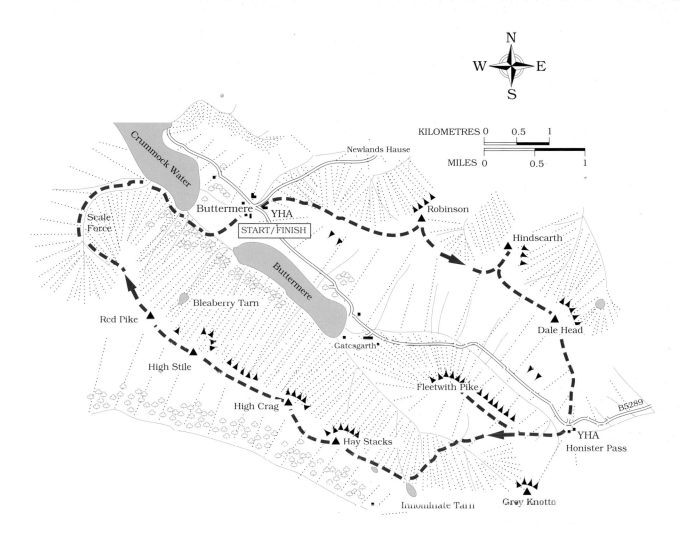

KILOMETRES 0   0.5   1

MILES 0   0.5   1

ALONG THE WAY

Buttermere consists of a few farms, two hotels and a scattering of stone cottages. It's an old farming community and the name, meaning 'the lake beside the pastures', refers to the small area of land that separates Crummock Water from Buttermere. The tiny church in Buttermere is particularly charming and dates from the thirteenth century. It sits on raised ground with a fine view over the area. At **Dubs Quarry** there's a mountain refuge that has been renovated from one of the old mine buildings. Here the quarry men would live during the week only going home on Saturday night before returning back to work on Monday morning. These days it's walkers, hikers and mountaineers who return to the hut each weekend for pleasure rather than work.

Hay Stacks failed to qualify as one of Wainwright's 'best half-dozen fells' due to its altitude of only 579m (1900ft). But although it may be short in height it more than makes up for this in its sheer beauty and its magnificent views to Pillar and Great Gable. Wainwright therefore described Hay Stacks as the 'best fell-top of all' and on his death his ashes were scattered on this fell.

Scale Force is the longest waterfall in the Lake District at 38m (125ft). The falls are hidden in a narrow tree-lined cleft and are visited during the descent of this walk. William Wordsworth described them as, 'a slender stream faintly illuminating a gloomy fissure'.

Overleaf: Buttermere Lake with High Crag and High Stile

21

A CIRCUIT OF CRUMMOCK WATER AND LOWESWATER

This walk takes in two of Lakeland's lakes, Loweswater and Crummock Water, which lie beyond Buttermere in the far north-west of the district. This is a relatively remote corner and the lakes are often peaceful and still, with large reed beds dominating the shoreline of Loweswater. The woods that surround the lake are rich with wildlife, while the hills are full of contrasts, with those to the west being of modest height and mostly grass covered, while to the east they are higher, more rugged and more spectacular in every way. Crummock Water is the largest lake in the Buttermere valley and it dominates the scene with views of it available throughout this tour. Perhaps more than any walk in the Lake District this is one of high contrast, taking in many different facets of Lakeland scenery.

DAY ONE

Starting from the northern end of Loweswater lake, a bridleway takes you through Iredale Place to a T-junction, where you turn south-east and begin the long walk up Burnbank Fell. You are drawn around the lower slopes of Burnbank Fell into Holme Beck, before you may leave the bridleway and walk up to the summit of Burnbank Fell. There aren't many paths to follow leaving you to pick your own way to the top. But with views growing over Loweswater, there's plenty of reason to stop and rest while you take in the scene. Burnbank Fell forms the cornerstone of the Loweswater Fells and provides clear views west over the Lake District National Park boundary.

WALK FACTS

Start/Finish	Loweswater, GR 116225
Distance	Day one: 18km (11 miles)
	Day two: 20km (12.4 miles)
Total ascent	Day one: 900m (2952ft)
	Day two: 1250m (4101ft)
Time	Day one: 7 hours
	Day two: 8 hours

Difficulty A straightforward fell walk, sometimes with only faint paths to follow, so some navigational skills are needed

Accommodation Youth hostel, B&Bs, campsites and hotel at Buttermere, limited B&Bs and hotels around Loweswater

Public transport There's no public transport to the start of the walk as described but there are infrequent bus services to Buttermere from Keswick, which is also linked to the railway stations at Windermere and Penrith

Walk south from Burnbank Fell over rolling grass to Blake Fell, the highest of the Loweswater Fells, with a splendid array of mountains in view, from Skiddaw and Blencathra in the north-east to Scafell in the south-east. An old boundary fence guides you south-east to Gavel Fell, where the boundary markers are interlaced with wire fencing to identify district boundary lines.

There's a change of direction now as you head for Loweswater village, by walking north-east to Black Crag, until you can swing north-east around the top of the crags and drop down easily to High Nook Farm. A short walk takes you to Loweswater village, with its church, pub and a scattering of farms and cottages. For those in need of a pint of fine Jennings ale, the Kirkstile Inn is highly recommended.

Your next objective is Mellbreak and the climb begins by walking out of Loweswater and over Church Bridge past Kirkhead Farm. At the head of the lane a path tackles Mellbreak, climbing steeply over heather and crags. On the summit plateau a pronounced depression separates the twin tops. For the best views over Crummock Water, walk north-east to the edge of the fell, with Grasmoor showing its finest aspect to Mellbreak and the western observer.

Descend from the southern top of Mellbreak,

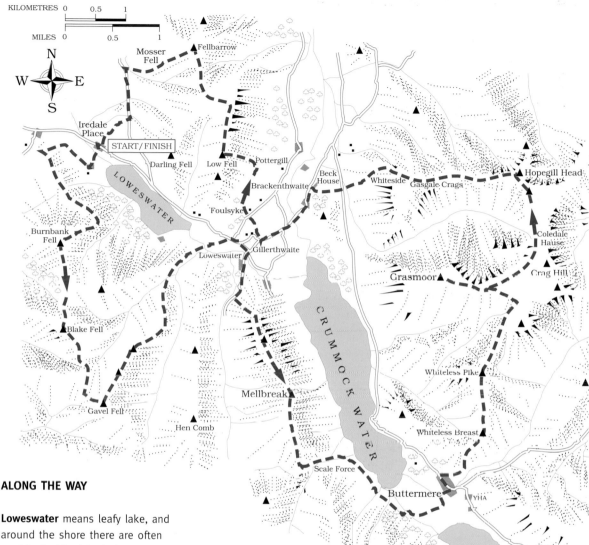

KILOMETRES 0   0.5   1

MILES 0   0.5   1

N
W   E
S

Mosser
Fell

Fellbarrow

Iredale
Place

START / FINISH

Darling Fell   Low Fell   Pottergill

Beck
House

Whiteside   Gasgale Crags

Hopegill Head

Brackenthwaite

LOWESWATER

Foulsyke

Burnbank
Fell

Loweswater   Gillerthwaite

Coledale
Hause

Grasmoor

Crag Hill

Blake Fell

CRUMMOCK WATER

Whiteless Pike

Mellbreak

Gavel Fell

Hen Comb

Whiteless Breast

Scale Force

Buttermere

YHA

ALONG THE WAY

Loweswater means leafy lake, and around the shore there are often reed beds. The lake is just over a mile long and half a mile wide, with a maximum depth of 18m (60ft). Unlike all the other lakes in the Lake District, its waters flow inwards, towards the centre of the region.

Crummock Water is the largest of the three lakes in this area, measuring around 2½ miles long, over half a mile wide and 44m (144ft) deep. At one time Crummock Water and Buttermere were linked, and some suspect that

Loweswater may also have been linked to this chain. The three lakes are now separated by narrow strips of flat meadow land, where today the small villages of Loweswater and Buttermere exist, although during long periods of heavy rain these areas often flood. This whole area is very rich in wildlife, insects, woodland and lakeside plants: the red squirrel can often be seen high on the northern shore of Crummock

Water, in Lanthwaite Wood.
Buttermere village made the national news in 1802 when it was discovered that one of the villagers, Mary Robinson, had been tricked into marriage by a man calling himself the Hon. Augustus Hope. He turned out to be a rogue, an impostor and bigamist. The story became the subject of several plays and Mary Robinson became known as the Maid of Buttermere.

over Scale Knott to Scale Beck, which is crossed leaving you to walk along the shore of Crummock Water to Buttermere village, where ample accommodation awaits.

DAY TWO

The high-level fell walk back to the start begins with a steep haul up Whiteless Breast to Whiteless Pike from Buttermere. A path leaves the western end of the village, leading behind cottages and onto the open fell. The view builds over Buttermere, Crummock Water and Loweswater as you climb, with the rugged escarpment of the High Stile Ridge looking particularly spectacular.

Wonderful Lakeland ridge walking leads over Wandope and to Crag Hill. At the hollow between Crag Hill and Grasmoor, turn west around the edge of the plateau to Grasmoor's summit, which is marked by a huge heap of stones, while a small wind-break nearby provides the better views.

Head east from Grasmoor to Coledale Hause before clawing your way uphill over the shale slopes of Hopegill Head, with steep, unstable crags tumbling north from its summit cairn. A classic traverse leads

View west over Crummock Water

west along the arm of Gasgale Crags to Whiteside. The summit is perched at the end of the ridge overlooking the steep, west-facing crags, with magnificent panoramic views across the coastal plains of Cumbria.

A steep descent takes you north-west and then west to Beck House and on to Pickett Howe through woods to a road. Pick your way through the lanes until you can finally begin your climb to Fellbarrow by taking a path that climbs from Pottergill straight up to Low Fell; although at 423m (1388ft) this is the highest point in this small group of fells. To end the day, grassland provides easy walking to Sourfoot Fell and Smithy Fell, while field paths and stiles provide access to the summit of Fellbarrow. A stone trig point marks the summit, with a superb view to the south-east, which includes Skiddaw, Blencathra, Grasmoor, Bowfell, Great Gable and Scafell Pike. The final descent of the day is west over Mosser Fell to a short track that leads to a gate and the Mosser Road. Here you must turn left to follow the road back to the start of the walk in Lorton Vale.

KESWICK TO BUTTERMERE

The North-Western Fells provide some of the finest views over Derwent Water, Borrowdale, Buttermere and beyond, while it may also claim some of the finest walking and some of the most shapely summits in the Lake District. This walk encircles the Newlands valley on its journey between Keswick and Buttermere. Along the way it takes in the classic traverse of Cat Bells and the summit of Dale Head, with its sweeping view down the length of the Newlands valley to Skiddaw. The return journey includes Crag Hill where a broad plateau is edged with steep crags, and Causey Pike, the slender ridge of which provides delightful walking through bilberry before the scamper home through the valley begins.

WALK FACTS

Start/Finish	Keswick, GR 266234
Distance	Day one: 18km (11 miles)
	Day two: 12km (7.5 miles)
Total ascent	Day one: 750m (2460ft)
	Day two: 850m (2789ft)
Time	Day one: 7 hours
	Day two: 5½ hours

Difficulty A medium-length walk over high fells with clear paths throughout but some steep climbs
Accommodation B&Bs, hotels, campsites and youth hostels at Keswick and Buttermere
Public transport Regular bus services link Keswick with railway stations at Windermere and Penrith. Infrequent bus services extend to Buttermere

Grisedale Pike from Crag Hill

DAY ONE

You need to pick your way along road, lanes and footpaths, before you can set foot on the fells, but it's an easy walk. You begin opposite the Pencil Museum in Keswick, from where a path leads over the River Derwent to Portinscale and past the entrance to Nicol End. A woodland walk through Fawe Woods leads to Hawse End below Cat Bells.

At last you can climb a hill! The path onto Cat Bells is clear, though steep to begin with. Along the way you pass a plaque set in the rock commemorating Arthur Leonard, the founder of Co-operative and Communal Holidays, who died in 1948. The broad path winds along this famous ridge to Maiden Moor, although you'll bypass the highest point and the best views if you stick too rigidly to the path. So bag the summit and then take a peek over the cliff edge for views of the Newlands valley and some of its disused mine workings.

Further along this broad ridge a steep climb leads to the cairned summit of High Spy, with more views down the Newlands valley and to Dale Head, which will be climbed next. A steep descent to Dalehead Tarn leaves you to reclaim all that lost height to stand at the summit of Dale Head. For your thigh-burning efforts, you are amply rewarded though with a well-built cairn and a view that sweeps from your feet down the Newlands valley to Skiddaw.

Some wonderful high-level ridge walking awaits as you are left to wander along the narrowing ridge of Hindscarth Edge, with views over Honister to Fleetwith Pike, Pillar and Great Gable. A short diversion at a grassy hause takes you to Hindscarth's rocky summit, where a nearby wind-break marks the

Rowling End leading to Causey Pike seen from Cat Bells

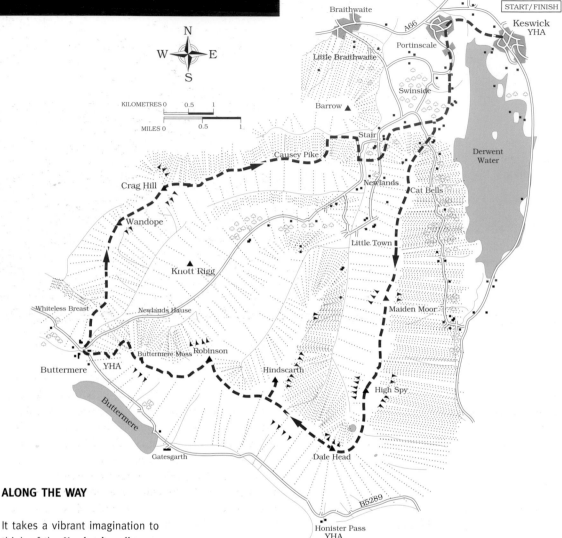

ALONG THE WAY

It takes a vibrant imagination to think of the **Newlands valley** as the focus of a mining industry, but for more than 2,000 years these hills have been mined for their rich deposits of copper, lead and silver. Some of the smelting works that existed in this area were the largest in England, if not in Europe in their time. Today the mines have closed but there are traces of the industry that helped to bring prosperity to Keswick. In particular the track that leads down the Newlands valley was built to serve the mines and processing works

that once existed at Copperheap Bay and Silver Hill before going on to one of the seven smelt-works around the Keswick area.

Cat Bells is a very popular fell as it provides extensive views across Derwent Water to Keswick, and of Skiddaw and Blencathra towering overhead. There are also views to Bassenthwaite Lake, down the length of Borrowdale and to Causey Pike and Grisedale Pike in the north-western fells. No wonder then that the famous guidebook

writer, the late Alfred Wainwright, described this fell as, 'One of the very best of the shorter climbs'. Few would disagree!

Many walkers, including Wainwright, refer to **Crag Hill** as **Eel Crag**, but the OS gives it the name Crag Hill, while the crags to the north of the summit are called Eel Crag. Whatever the correct name, the fell lies at the heart of the north-western fells, with ridges and valleys radiating from its massive bulk.

location of the finest views, which include the fells of Wandope, Crag Hill and Sail.

Leaving Hindscarth by the way you came, slender Littledale Edge leads onto Robinson where your views extend down into Buttermere, Crummock Water and Loweswater. At sunset the view is all the more delicious, but you must come down sometime and the path leads over High Snockrigg to Buttermere.

DAY TWO

It has been a great walk getting to Buttermere and the walk back to Keswick is just as splendid. Whiteless Pike, Wandope and Crag Hill lie on the agenda and extensive views are to be expected. From Buttermere, a path climbs north-east along the banks of Mill Beck through woods and onto the open fell. The way ahead is clear and easy, other than being continually uphill of course! Whiteless Breast and Whiteless Pike both bring early rewards with views to Buttermere, Crummock Water and the towering High Stile Ridge. The slender arm of Whiteless Edge, isn't anywhere near as narrow as its name suggests but it has one or two awkward steps to negotiate before an easier path takes you over Wandope, with a big haul onto the broad plateau of Crag Hill ahead. At the heart of the north-western fells, it's a splendid hill, thanks to it being located at the hub of radiating ridges and being surrounded by fells.

Buttermere from High Stile to Robinson (with snow)

One of the finest arms of Crag Hill stretches east over Sail and Causey Pike to the Newlands valley and this is used during the return to Keswick. The ridge is justly popular and forms part of the classic Coledale Horseshoe, one of the great walks of Lakeland. The going is fairly easy, although a rough and rocky descent from Crag Hill may have you thinking otherwise. But the difficulties are short-lived, leaving you to walk on clear paths over Sail and down to Sail Pass. Here, a fork in the path could be confusing, so stay right to climb Scar Crags with its craggy southern slopes. Even though higher than Causey Pike by 35m (115ft), Scar Crags comes second to Causey Pike in most people's minds. This is due to the prominence of Causey Pike and its distinctive form when viewed from the east, while Scar Crags is merely an extension of its ridge that leads to Crag Hill.

Stay on the path to Causey Pike, its summit instantly giving more satisfaction than its neighbour, and then descend steeply over Rowling End to the road at Stonycroft. Paths and lanes lead to Rowling End Farm, across Newlands Beck to Ghyll Bank and on to Skelgill. A short walk deposits you back at the car park at the base of Cat Bells from where the outward journey can be retraced to Keswick.

COCKERMOUTH TO BUTTERMERE

The far north-western corner of the Lake District is bypassed by many walkers so this walk takes advantage of this and makes a traverse of Lorton Vale from Cockermouth to Buttermere. Lorton Vale divides the Fellbarrow group from the Whinlatter and Grasmoor fells. The valley is broad and flat with a winding river and a rich pasture. There's a scattering of cottages and hamlets but it is Cockermouth that is the centre of human population here. Many of the fells are rarely walked, with only faint sheep tracks through the grass. But as you move closer to Buttermere the fells become well tramped with clear paths blazing your route up to Grasmoor. This is a walk of variety and contrast, from the busy town of Cockermouth through the quiet fringe of the Lake District. You enter the popular heart of Buttermere before retreating north-west once more to Cockermouth over the quiet and remote Whinlatter fells.

DAY ONE

Cockermouth is Wordsworth's town: he was born here in 1770 and spent the first fifteen years of his life at Wordsworth House on the main street along with his sister Dorothy and their brothers Richard, John and Christopher. So even though Cockermouth stands outside the Lake District National Park boundary it is very popular with tourists. But you only have to walk south from the town into Lorton Vale to discover an almost unknown valley.

You leave busy Cockermouth by tracing the River Cocker that bisects the centre of the town. A footpath traces the river as it escapes the town and passes under the A66 into the farming valley of Lorton Vale. The footpath leaves the river bank for a route through the vast, flat pasture between the River Cocker and the B5289. Ahead, the fells grow in stature as you arrive at Low Lorton, a small cluster of cottages. Wordsworthians come here to try and find the Lorton Yew, as Wordsworth wrote a poem about this tree that stands at neighbouring High Lorton.

A short stretch of road walking is needed to reach the base of the fells, as both footpaths in the valley and on the neighbouring fells are very limited in Lorton Vale. So trace the quiet lane along the base of the Fellbarrow group of fells to Thackthwaite where you can take a footpath onto the fell. It's a steep climb onto the grassland that provides easy walking to Sourfoot Fell and Smithy Fell, while field paths and stiles provide access to the summit of Fellbarrow.

WALK FACTS

Start/Finish	Cockermouth, GR 125305
Distance	Day one: 21km (13 miles)
	Day two: 22km (13.7 miles)
Total ascent	Day one: 750m (2460ft)
	Day two: 1200m (3937ft)
Time	Day one: 8 hours
	Day two: 9 hours

Difficulty A straightforward but long fell walk with a lot of ascent on day two. Most of the paths are clear but some are only faint, so some navigational skills are needed

Accommodation Youth hostel, B&Bs, hotels and campsites at Buttermere and Cockermouth

Public transport Infrequent bus services to Buttermere from Keswick, which is also linked to the railway stations at Windermere and Penrith. Cockermouth is well served with bus services from Keswick, with connections to the railway station at Penrith

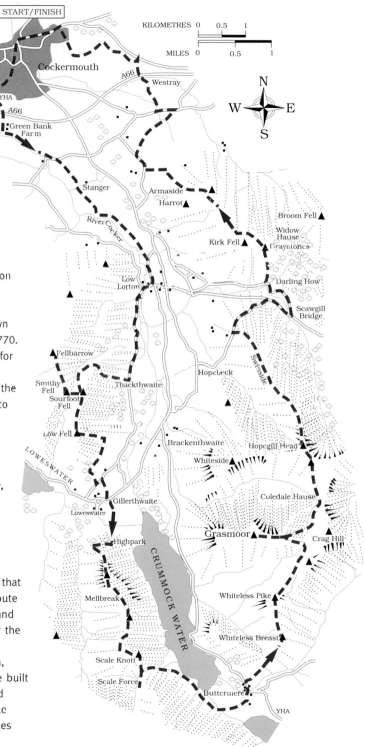

Left: *View over Crummock Water to Fellbarrow*

ALONG THE WAY

Fell walkers rarely walk further north-west than Loweswater as the **Lorton Valley** is devoid of lofty summits. It is instead a vale of farmland with meadows, pasture and a sprinkling of farms and cottages. Lorton Hall has a large pele-tower which reflects that this is open country with little protection from hills, so the pele-tower was built to guard against attack.

William Wordsworth was born at what is now known as Wordsworth House in Cockermouth on 7 April 1770. The house is a Georgian town house built in 1745 for Joshua Lucock, sheriff of Cumberland. Later it was owned by John Wordsworth, William's father. Today the house is owned by the National Trust and is open to the public.

Lorton Yew stands at High Lorton on the banks of Whit Beck in a field next to a telephone kiosk. Wordsworth wrote of it in 1804:

> *There is a Yew Tree, pride of Lorton in the vale,*
> *Which to this day stands single, in the midst*
> *Of its own darkness, as it stood of yore...*

A **Roman road** extended from Papcastle near Cockermouth down Lorton Vale before rising over Whinlatter Pass to Keswick and the Roman forts in that area of the Lake District. Whinlatter was also the route taken by the turnpike road between Cockermouth and Keswick. The road was built along with others after the 1762 Turnpike Act to link the industrial and market centres of Cockermouth, Hesket Newmarket, Penrith, Keswick, Windermere and Kendal. These roads were built to improve transport for landowners, merchants and manufacturers and they were maintained by turnpike trusts to ensure that hedges were cut back, pot-holes were filled and drainage ditches provided.

33

Below: Hopegill Head summit from the north-west ridge

A stone trig point marks the summit, with its superb views to the south and east, which include Skiddaw, Blencathra, Grasmoor, Bowfell, Great Gable and Scafell Pike.

You must retrace your steps to Sourfoot Fell and then follow the grassy ridge Low Fell which at 423m (1388ft) is the highest point in this small group. A steep path descends back into Lorton Vale and the hamlet of Gillerthwaite and Loweswater soon comes underfoot. But you are not in the valley long, for a climb onto Mellbreak awaits. The path is steep but your efforts are rewarded with two pronounced tops and fine views over Crummock Water to Grasmoor. Descend from the southern top of Mellbreak, over Scale Knott to Scale Beck, which is crossed leaving you to walk along the shore of Crummock Water to Buttermere village.

DAY TWO

Buttermere lies at the heart of the fells, with steep slopes leading to celebrated lofty tops on all sides. But unlike most walkers in Buttermere you will be turning your back on many of the famous heights for a moment as you head for the quiet Whinlatter Fells and Cockermouth. But you do get to sample Grasmoor on the walk and the climb begins with a steep haul up Whiteless Breast to Whiteless Pike. The view builds over Buttermere, Crummock Water and Loweswater as you climb, with the rugged escarpment of the High Stile Ridge looking particularly spectacular from this angle. Superb ridge walking leads over Wandope to Grasmoor's summit, which is marked by a huge heap of stones, while a small wind-break nearby provides fine views which extend down the length of Lorton Vale.

Head east from Grasmoor to Coledale Hause before walking up to Hopegill Head, with steep unstable crags tumbling north from its summit cairn. Again there is a spectacular view, this time north-north-west, down the long arm of Hopegill Head to Swinside and the Whinlatter forests, beyond which poke the bald summits of Kirk Fell, Broom Fell and Lord's Seat. The descent towards these remote fells begins with a steep scramble, but soon you are tracing a wall down the ridge and then you drop off the end of the fell to a quiet narrow lane. Follow the lane east towards the Whinlatter Pass. You join the B5292, turn sharp left to Scawgill Bridge from where a path climbs through Whinlatter Forest to Graystones and Kirk Fell. Slopes tumble away to the north-west and you'll pick up a path that drops over these quiet and rarely walked fells to another lane near Armaside. The fell walking is over, leaving you to link lanes and footpaths to Westray from where a footpath crosses the A66, leaves the Lake District National boundary and enters Cockermouth.

BASSENTHWAITE LAKE SKYLINE

The far north-western corner of the Lake District is often disregarded by walkers, for Skiddaw and many of the surrounding fells lack the craggy grandeur of many of Lakeland's more popular mountains. But there are some wonderful rolling fells in the area that are ideally placed to be combined into a circuit of Bassenthwaite Lake. In particular this walk shows that Skiddaw, Sale Fell, Ling Fell, Broom Fell and Lord's Seat all have as much to offer in terms of walking experience as spectacular Hopegill Head and Grisedale Pike. At the end of the walk you will have traversed the skyline of Bassenthwaite Lake and had the chance to view it from every angle.

WALK FACTS

Start/Finish	Braithwaite, GR 231237
Distance	Day one: 17.7km (11 miles)
	Day two: 24km (15 miles)
Total ascent	Day one: 950m (3117ft)
	Day two: 1100m (3609ft)
Time	Day one: 7 hours
	Day two: 8 hours

Difficulty A long high-level fell walk on paths and tracks with lots of ups and downs on day two. Some pathless terrain where good navigational skills will be required

Accommodation B&Bs, hotels and campsites at Braithwaite, Keswick and Bassenthwaite, youth hostel at Keswick

Public transport Regular bus services to Keswick from Penrith and Windermere railway stations. Bus services extend from Keswick to Bassenthwaite

Bassenthwaite Lake from Sale Fell

DAY ONE

Day two is long, so to make the trip more equally balanced you should start from Braithwaite rather than Keswick. But no matter where you begin Skiddaw is your first target. So walk past the Keswick Youth Hostel, under the bed of the dismantled railway line to Briar Rigg, from where you follow a signpost 'Public Bridleway Skiddaw' over the A66 to the Latrigg car park. Having escaped the town you walk between fields and around the western flank of Lonscale Fell to gain Jenkin Hill, with the valley floor now a long way below. Little Man soon comes underfoot with its fine view over Derwent Water.

Stay on the main path to Skiddaw's summit where a plaque identifies some of the tops to be seen from this, Lakeland's fourth highest mountain. According to its rock formations it is also the oldest mountain in the region. Its slates and shale are marine deposits which were formed long before the volcanic rock found in the central fells.

You now get a chance to experience a lesser-known side of Skiddaw as you descend north to Broad End and down to Bakestall to join the main Skiddaw House access track near Whitewater Dash. The access track leads down to the road near Peter House Farm and a bridleway continues to Bassenthwaite village.

DAY TWO

To get to the hills from Bassenthwaite village you must follow roads and lanes over the A591 main road, along the B5291 and over the A66. Walk straight across the road to the Pheasant Inn. A footpath about half a mile west along the road from the inn leads

Opposite: Summit of Hopegill Head

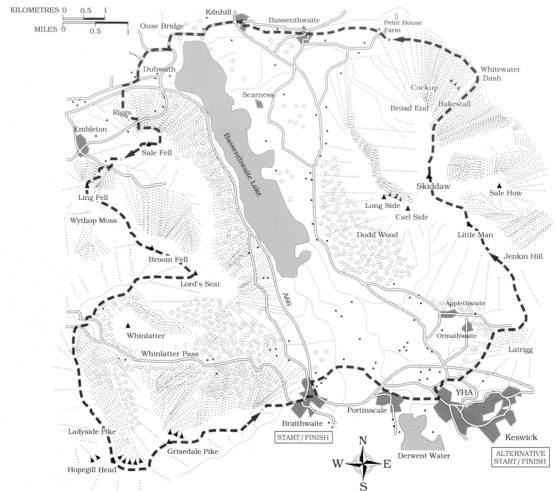

ALONG THE WAY

Bassenthwaite Lake's eastern side is dominated by Skiddaw, the fourth highest peak in the Lake District at 930m (3053ft) above sea-level. On Skiddaw's western side, overlooking the lake, is Dodd, described by Wainwright as 'a whelp of Skiddaw crouched at the feet of its parent'. But unlike Skiddaw, Dodd is cloaked in spruce, fir and pine. Bassenthwaite village is located near the lake of the same name, with many of its houses grouped around a small green. The church of

St John, built in 1878, stands half a mile south of the village.

The **Whinlatter Forest Park** is an area where tourism and industry exist hand in hand. There's a visitor's centre and an extensive network of marked paths and trails for walkers, orienteers and mountain bikers. A useful map showing the area in detail is available from the visitor's centre, making this a popular destination for families. Few venture far from the forest paths, however, and the fells to the north of the forest

boundary are rarely visited. The excellent road through Whinlatter Forest, the Whinlatter Pass, provides fine views over the eastern end of Bassenthwaite Lake to Skiddaw.

Hopegill Head may be overshadowed by Grisedale Pike as far as pure altitude goes, but it has an impressive range of cliffs that sweep away from its summit and supporting ridges. The approach to the summit from Ladyside Pike brings views that capture the immensity of Hopegill Head, adding a spectacular finale to the climb.

onto Sale Fell, which marks the cornerstone of the North-Western Fells. You get views into the idyllic Wythop valley with its green fields and farm resting in seclusion between Sale Fell and Ling Fell, but your eye will no doubt be drawn to Hopegill Head and Grisedale Pike, your final objectives of the day. Skiddaw to the east looks particularly impressive from this unusual angle and far from the boring hill that so many people believe it to be.

Leave Sale Fell by descending west to Wythop valley where you can follow a broad track onto Ling Fell, with its trig point rising from a sea of heather. Then descend across the deep and soggy hollow of Wythop Moss along the line of an ancient path to Widow Hause and finally Broom Fell. An impressive stone cairn by a fence seems to mark the summit, until you study the map more closely and realise that the highest point lies on a small mound to the south-east of the cairn. The highest fell in this group of hills, north of Whinlatter Pass, is Lord's Seat. It comes underfoot after a walk along a wide and grassy ridge. There's no cairn and no seat but the view is outstanding and includes Bassenthwaite Lake once more.

Before you can climb another mountain you must descend, by walking south-west towards the Aiken Plantation and down past Darling How to the B5292 Whinlatter Pass road. A short stretch of road work takes you over Blaze Beck towards High Lorton. It's then a long climb up the north-west ridge of Hopegill Head via Swinside, from where the ridge begins to narrow as you trace a stone wall over heather slopes to Ladyside Pike. This in itself is a worthwhile summit with airy views across to Grisedale Pike and a narrow ridge leading to Hopegill Head. An impressive though not difficult ridge continues south with a final short pull taking you over the northern crags of Hopegill Head. The summit cairn is perched very near the edge of the crag to allow sweeping views. With the day drawing to a close and the sun setting over to the west, it's time to begin the final descent, this time to Braithwaite via Grisedale Pike. The path sticks closely to the cliffs of Hobcarton Crags before rising steeply, too steeply for this time of day in fact, to Grisedale Pike. This is a stunning viewpoint at any time but particularly so after this walk, for it includes Bassenthwaite Lake and Skiddaw, two of the main features of the journey. Finally you descend to Braithwaite, with the sun setting over the Whinlatter Fells and Bassenthwaite Lake to the west.

WASDALE SKYLINE

The Wasdale valley is renowned as a base from which to explore Lakeland's finest and most rugged rocky mountains. All the classics are here including Pillar, Great Gable, Scafell and Scafell Pike. With its many crags and rocky mountains, it is perhaps no surprise that Wasdale became the cradle of Lakeland rock climbing when the pioneers first realised the enjoyment, excitement and adventure that the sport could provide. But there's more to Wasdale than the popular favourites already mentioned, for the lower fells of Middle Fell, Seatallan, Haycock and Illgill Head are all fine mountains in their own way and they provide an important final chapter to the Wasdale story. So this walk captures the complete Wasdale skyline as it takes in just about every major fell along the way.

WALK FACTS

Start/Finish	Wast Water Youth Hostel, Wasdale Hall, GR 145045
Distance	Day one: 22km (13.7 miles)
	Day two: 19km (11.5 miles)
Total ascent	Day one: 1850m (6069ft)
	Day two: 1600m (5249ft)
Time	Day one: 10 hours
	Day two: 8 hours

Difficulty A long walk with more than average amount of ascent over rocky, mountainous terrain and the highest fells of England

Accommodation Youth hostel at Wasdale Hall, B&Bs, hotel and campsites at Wasdale Head. B&Bs at Nether Wasdale

Public transport No public transport services extend to Wasdale. The nearest railway station is at Seascale, from where bus services extend to Gosforth

Previous page: Great Gable seen from Great End

DAY ONE

You could begin this walk from anywhere in the Wasdale valley, but the youth hostel at the western end of the lake is perhaps the ideal kick-off point, with its stunning view down the length of the valley to Great Gable plugging the head of the valley like a giant Egyptian pyramid. Begin by road walking to Greendale Farm on the Gosforth road, from where a path heads for the lower slopes of Middle Fell. The summit of Middle Fell is grossly under-appreciated, as it offers splendid views down the lake and is often well below the cloud when its neighbours are hidden. A gentle descent continues towards Haycock, but with Seatallan so close, it's worth making a diversion from the direct route. This is another underrated fell, and although I must confess it's not one of my favourites, it does have its own unique appeal and gives good views from its broad summit dome.

Finally Haycock comes underfoot and this is surely one of Wasdale's forgotten gems, with its rugged cliffs to the north, extensive views and very respectable height of 798m (2618ft). In any other region, Haycock would be popular but in Wasdale it's somewhat overshadowed. A stone wall leads to Scoat Fell, which again is rarely climbed for its own end, as its neighbours are far more favourable objectives. In particular there's Steeple, the highest point of which rises from a slender rocky rib that extends north from Scoat Fell. The summit brings views down Ennerdale and over Mirk Cove to Pillar.

You have now crossed the divide from the smooth grassy contours around Middle Fell and Haycock to the rocky, crag-ridden slopes of Pillar. The summit of Pillar is broad and flat and not as impressive as its name might suggest. The broad ridge of the mountain continues in an easterly direction to Black Sail Pass with the Black Sail Youth Hostel, down to the left at the head of Ennerdale, one of the most remote buildings in England. Kirk Fell comes next with a clear path leading between crags to its twinned-topped summit, with two neighbouring tarns punctuating the plateau. From the second summit on Kirk Fell you can walk down to Beck Head and climb almost immediately up Great Gable. The climb is a long and arduous haul over scree and rock but the views from the top to Wasdale are unsurpassed in the Lake District, and you will also be able to take in virtually the complete route of your walk, including tomorrow's section over Scafell Pike.

It will now be late in the day, so descend to Sty Head and walk down to Wasdale Head for a night of rest in a campsite, B&B or hotel.

DAY TWO

To make the walk as complete as possible, retrace your steps back up to Sty Head and from here you can tackle the Scafell massif by following the Corridor Route. This follows an upwardly slanting shelf that cuts through the western flank of the mountain in quite spectacular fashion, when you remember that this is the highest land in England. The path leads across the mouth of Skew Gill, over the end of Greta Gill and below the rocky knob of Round How before crossing the head of Piers Gill and finally emerging at Lingmell Col. You are now faced with a long haul up a clearly defined path to the summit of Scafell Pike, the highest point in England at 977m (3205ft). But don't just stick to the summit cairn, as you'll find the best views by peering over the cliffs to Upper Eskdale and Scafell.

Crossing from Scafell Pike to Scafell, the route follows a descent down the scree of Mickledore, below the towering cliffs of Scafell's east buttress. You then follow a narrow path past Foxes Tarn to the summit of Scafell, with its premier views to Scafell Pike, Great Gable and the whole of the Lake District.

A westerly descent over Green How takes you to the edge of Burnmoor Tarn, from where a path climbs onto Illgill Head. Steep cliffs line the summit ridge and these lead to the famous screes that tumble into Wast Water. The ridge leads easily to Whin Rigg, but take time to turn around to take in the views back to Wasdale Head, with the sun setting over Pillar perhaps.

The day ends with a descent down the bank of Greathall Gill to the valley floor near the shores of Wast Water, only a short walk from the start at the youth hostel.

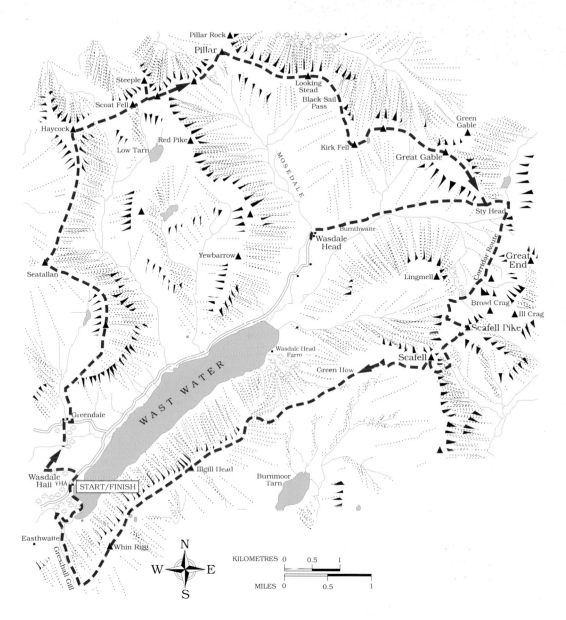

ALONG THE WAY

Pillar's name originates from Pillar Rock, which is a pillar-like tower of rock rising to the north of the mountain. You can gain a view of it by scampering a short way down a path to the north of the summit. To gain the summit itself you must use climbing skills.

Great Gable's highest point is marked with a memorial plaque commemorating those members of the Fell & Rock Climbing Club who died in World War I. About 100m from the summit, overlooking Wasdale Head, there's Westmorland Cairn, which provides unrivalled views down the lake. The cairn was built by two brothers in 1876 to mark what they thought was the finest view in the Lake District. Most people will no doubt agree with their opinion.

Scafell, although less popular than Scafell Pike, has much of interest and is England's premier mountain crag for rock climbers. It was originally thought to be the highest of the Scafell range, while the lower, neighbouring summits were collectively known simply as the Scafell Pikes. But Scafell is still the major summit in some ways, as you get a real feeling of mankind's insignificance here when compared to the huge range of mountains that are laid out around you.

ESKDALE TO WASDALE

The Burnmoor and Miterdale area consists of rough moorland where ghostly legends are allowed to run riot, for it was here that an old corpse road once existed over which coffins were carried on horseback between Wasdale and the consecrated ground at Eskdale. This has given rise to tales of ghosts, hauntings and mysterious happenings over the years, but this is all part of the rich Lakeland saga and perhaps the place is all the more inviting for having these legends.

Today Scafell Pike dominates the scene leaving these moors rarely visited and a peaceful place where a walker can escape the summer influx of visitors. In particular these moors are ideally placed to be combined with a crossing between Eskdale and Wasdale. But as a change is as good as a rest this two-day journey combines the famous rocky heights of Scafell and Scafell Pike with the less famous moors of Burnmoor and Miterdale.

DAY ONE

The Ravenglass and Eskdale Railway provides a unique and useful means of reaching the mountains. The small train puffs through Eskdale from Ravenglass with open-top carriages and the whiff of hot oil, steam and coal in the air. The journey ends at Dalegarth Station and from here you are on foot to Wasdale via England's highest mountain, Scafell Pike.

A number of paths leave Eskdale for Scafell Pike. This route traces the footpath that leaves Eskdale near the Woolpack Inn and climbs up to Eel Tarn. This is a rugged and knobbly landscape, with a colony of black-headed gulls often in residence at the tarn. A green track continues to Stony Tarn which is set in a wide depression. The path continues towards Scafell via Slight Side and although this is a long climb, the rocky ground of England's highest mountain massif soon comes underfoot. The summit of Scafell brings particularly fine views to Great Gable and Lingmell, while Scafell Pike will be seen directly across the great void that separates these two mountains. Although there are more adventurous routes, the laden backpacker is best advised to follow the Foxes Tarn path. This has been re-paved over recent years and is now a staircase of rock steps leading past the tiny pool of Foxes Tarn to the scree bank of Mickledore. Haul yourself up this scree to the narrow strip of land that is Mickledore and then Scafell Pike is well within striking distance.

WALK FACTS

Start/Finish	Dalegarth Station, Eskdale, GR 175007
Distance	Day one: 19.3km (12 miles)
	Day two: 17.7km (11 miles)
Total ascent	Day one: 1200m (3937ft)
	Day two: 700m (2297ft)
Time	Day one: 8 hours
	Day two: 7 hours

Difficulty A long walk over the highest mountains in England, but there are clear paths most of the way on day one. Day two is more remote and demands more care, but there is less hill climbing involved

Accommodation Youth hostels, B&Bs, hotels and campsites at Eskdale and Wasdale

Public transport The Ravenglass and Eskdale Railway extends down Eskdale to the start of this walk. There is no public transport to Wasdale

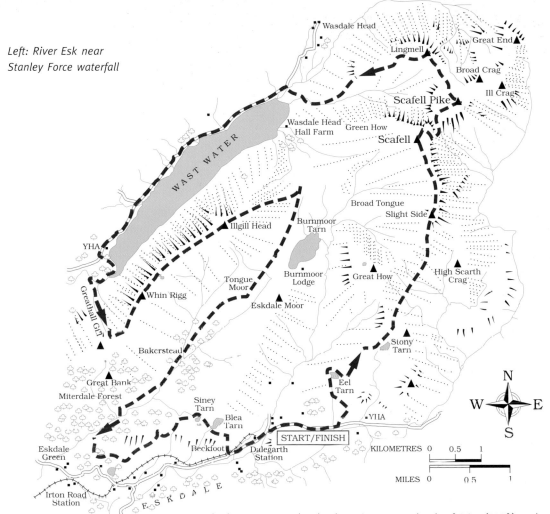

Left: River Esk near Stanley Force waterfall

ALONG THE WAY

Burnmoor Tarn stands on the Burnmoor Trod, an old corpse road that would have been used to carry the dead from the head of Wasdale to the nearest parish church in Eskdale, a distance of about 11km (7 miles) over some of the most desolate hill country in the Lake District. The coffins would have been strapped to sledges or horses.

There is a legend that while taking a dead man's body by horse to Eskdale, the horse bolted in the mist on a dark and stormy night, never to be seen again. The bearers had to return to the dead man's wife and tell of their misfortune. The woman died shortly after and her body was strapped to a horse to be carried to Eskdale. They encountered another storm on Burnmoor and the horse bolted with the woman's body and disappeared into the mist. The legend says that a ghostly horse bearing a coffin on its back may be seen during stormy nights on Burnmoor.

Wasdale claims to have the highest mountain, the deepest lake, the smallest church and the biggest liar in England. Scafell Pike is undoubtedly the highest mountain at 977m (3205ft) and Wast Water is the deepest lake at an average depth of 36m (118ft) and a maximum depth of 79m (260ft). But the claim of the smallest church is debatable as there are smaller churches around, although Wasdale's church is very tiny. Will Ritson, a famous wrestler in his youth, was the biggest liar and festivals are still held in his memory at Santon Bridge. Will Ritson's tales were laced with dry wit and sharpened by a judicious use of dialect. He is said to have won a lying competition outright by declaring himself unable to enter because he could not lie. He was mentioned in Victorian guidebooks and became a popular tourist attraction.

Wasdale can be clearly seen from Scafell Pike but there are plenty of routes that could be used to get off the mountain. I suggest Lingmell as the favoured option of descent, as it provides the most perfect views back to Scafell. I have often sat watching the final rays of sunlight casting their warm glow on the towering cliffs of Scafell before being forced to scamper down to the valley by torchlight.

The long ridge from Lingmell to Wasdale creates no navigational problems, but its gradient is far from kind on the knees. Once the valley is reached, there's a choice of accommodation at either end of the lake. But to keep day two as short as possible I suggest heading to the western end of Wast Water where a youth hostel is ideally placed for this walk.

DAY TWO

The return to Eskdale from Wasdale begins with a climb above the screes to Whin Rigg and Illgill Head. The screes are one of Wasdale's most famous features, as pink iron ore exists in the steep bank of crumbling rocks and this glows red, pink and orange under the setting sun and brings a rich variety of colour through the hanging weather and seasons.

Leaving the Youth Hostel, a path follows the lake shore through a wood to the outflow of Greathall Gill. A path clambers up the side of this watercourse and

Scafell from Lingmell with Wast Water on the right

this is followed until you are eventually deposited on the high fells once more. A gentle walk continues over the grass of Whin Rigg, from where the lip of the famous screes is traced. To the left the cliff edge is a mass of tumbling rocks, ravines with gullies and fragile buttresses. A steady pull takes you to Illgill Head, with its fine view to Wasdale Head marking your arrival.

Burnmoor Tarn lies in the valley to the right and you must now descend steeply to its shoreline. Burnmoor Lodge near the shore of the tarn was once a gamekeeper's lodge. From Burnmoor Tarn a direct return to Eskdale can be made by following the Old Corpse Road to Boot, now a bridleway. But to add a bit more distance to the walk, this route beats a retreat to Eskdale via Miterdale. The path sweeps down to the River Mite, which begins life high on Illgill Head, while the water of Burnmoor Tarn is drained down Whillan Beck directly to Boot and the River Esk.

The path through Miterdale leads over Tongue Moor and past Bakerstead. Before reaching Eskdale Green, the main path is left at Low Place where a final short hill climb takes you over Siney Tarn and Blea Tarn before reaching Beckfoot railway station, only one stop away from the Dalegarth Station on the Ravenglass to Eskdale Railway.

ENNERDALE HORSESHOE

The remote valley of Ennerdale is the centrepiece of this high-level circuit that scales just about every summit that overlooks the valley. The route is a popular single day's outing for some fit walkers, but it can also be enjoyed at a more leisurely pace if it is split between two days. Throughout the journey the walker traverses high ridges, clambers up steep rocky slopes and rises to some of Lakeland's most famous summits such as High Stile, Great Gable, Pillar and Hay Stacks. These ridges and mountains rise in sharp contrast to the smooth wooded slopes of Ennerdale and its broad valley bottom, which are never far from view and give walkers a continual point of interest from wherever they stand.

WALK FACTS

Start/Finish	Car park at western end of Ennerdale, GR 085154
Distance	Day one: 20km (12.4 miles)
	Day two: 22km (13.7 miles)
Total ascent	Day one: 1386m (4547ft)
	Day two: 1530m (5019ft)
Time	Day one: 8 hours
	Day two: 9 hours

Difficulty A long and strenuous walk that includes a lot of steep climbing over some of Lakeland's highest mountains

Accommodation Youth hostel at Gillerthwaite and Black Sail at the head of Ennerdale. Limited B&Bs around the western end of Ennerdale at Ennerdale Bridge

Public transport Railway station at Workington from where very limited bus services run to Ennerdale Bridge

DAY ONE

The fine viewpoint of Bowness Knott provides an early highlight to the day, revealing as it does famous views over Ennerdale and the walk ahead. Turning your back on the panorama for a moment, you are faced with a steep climb up the eastern bank of Rake Beck towards the summit of Great Borne. A shelter cairn, a trig point and panoramic views mark your arrival at this, the first summit of the day.

A high-level traverse along Ennerdale's northern skyline awaits, with a line of fencing making light work of the navigation to Starling Dodd with its distinctive cairn comprised of rock and iron fence posts. Ahead the distinctive red dome of Red Pike can be seen rising and from here the rounded slopes of Great Borne and Starling Dodd are replaced with the steep cliffs and hanging valleys that bite into the northern slopes of the High Stile Ridge, with spectacular views over Buttermere and the north-western range of fells. The walking is easy now and I usually find myself wandering around to take in all the views. Although this is a great walk it doesn't last long enough for me and all too soon the steep descent has to be made down to Scarth Gap, a notch between High Crag and Hay Stacks.

The rocks around Innominate Tarn on Hay Stacks were the final resting place of Wainwright's ashes, as this was his favourite fell. It may not have the height of its neighbours, but its situation brings spectacular views to the head of Ennerdale where Great Gable and Pillar dominate the skyline.

A long haul from Hay Stacks continues the walk around the head of Ennerdale to Brandreth from where Green Gable, with its stunning view down the length of Ennerdale, can be reached shortly. The final act on day one is to descend into Windy Gap and follow the path down into the head of Ennerdale, where accommodation can be found in the Black Sail Youth Hostel.

DAY TWO

The second half of the walk takes you down the southern side of Ennerdale, but first you must clamber back up to Windy Gap, using the route you descended down at the end of day one. Great Gable can then be

ENNERDALE HORSESHOE

Hikers on the High Stile Ridge. Buttermere below, Newlands Fells behind

climbed easily by the main path. Its summit brings views down the length of Wasdale, but its views to Ennerdale are disappointing when compared to the views from Green Gable. The emphasis returns to Ennerdale, as you walk from Great Gable to Beck Head and climb onto Kirk Fell. But again the views are somewhat disappointing, as Kirk Fell is a rather big lump with few cliff-edge views. Things improve as you descend to Black Sail Pass but with Pillar rising ahead the best is still to come. The main path takes you over Looking Stead to the summit of Pillar, but the finer alternative is to use the High Level Route, which makes a traverse of Pillar's northern face overlooking Ennerdale. The start of the path is marked by a small cairn on Looking Stead, from where a narrow path leads around the Ennerdale side of the mountain, continually rising and falling like a roller-coaster ride. At Robinson's Cairn you are greeted with stunning views down Ennerdale and across to the High Stile Ridge, but Pillar Rock is the main focus here. It is this rock that gives Pillar its name, as it is pillar-shaped when viewed from the

valley. Today it is a famous climbing crag, although scramblers too can reach its summit.

A steep path climbs from Pillar Rock to the summit of Pillar mountain. Its broad, open plateau provides a marked contrast to the confines of the High Level Route, with only a cairn, trig point and wind shelter punctuating the flat featureless expanse. Scoat Fell comes next, but it is Steeple that is the main focus of attention here, projecting like a finger from the main thrust of the mountain. A diversion to Steeple is well worth the effort, for the views back to Pillar and down the length of Ennerdale are unrivalled.

A boundary wall leads over Haycock, which ensures that you don't get lost, as the paths are less popular from now on and harder to trace on the ground. The homeward journey continues west and then north-west over the rolling fells above Iron Crag and Boathow Crag to a plantation beside Crag Fell. Here you can descend easily to Grike and then finally emerge at Crag Farm House and the shore of Ennerdale Water.

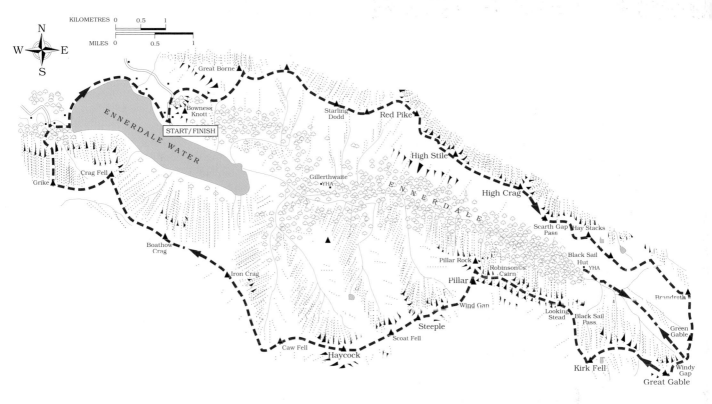

ALONG THE WAY

Coleridge and Wordsworth, two of Lakeland's most famous poets, visited **Ennerdale** during their famous 'Pikteresk Tour' of 1799. But the area has changed much since the late eighteenth century, though the head of Ennerdale is still a quiet, remote and lonely place. It remained a deer forest until the eighteenth century when its only dwellings were a couple of cottages at Gillerthwaite. But in the twentieth century the valley was drastically altered when the Forestry Commission planted extensive woods of conifers. This caused a great outcry and thankfully over recent years improved planting policies have provided a greater mix of species. Today there are a number of well-marked trails through the woods that begin from Bowness Knott.

Pillar Rock rises to the north of Pillar, giving the mountain its name. This independent column of rock is regarded by many as the most divine, most elegant and most aesthetic climbing cliff in England. The north-facing cliff is nearly 300m (984ft) high and is separated from Pillar mountain by a short spur. Pillar Rock is the only sizeable summit in the Lake District that cannot be climbed by simply walking. It was first climbed by a shepherd in 1826. The rock had been described as 'unclimbable' in the 1825 edition of Jonathan Otley's *Descriptive Guide to the Lake District* and a competition developed among the local dales folk to find who would be the first to stand on the top. On 9 July 1826 John Atkinson, a cooper from Crottfoot in Ennerdale scrambled to the top, making the first ascent. *The Cumberland Pacquet*, a local newspaper, informed its readers of the event, adding that, 'The only precaution he took for his descent was to place pieces of moss on the track by which he ascended'.

Robinson's Cairn, on the High Level Route of Pillar, is a memorial to energetic fell walker John Wilson Robinson. It is said he often walked from his home in Lorton over the Scarth Gap and Black Sail Passes to Wasdale Head, where he would join his friends for a day's rock climbing before walking all the way home again, a total distance of 38km (24 miles) excluding the walks to the climb!

WASDALE TO ENNERDALE

There is more to Wasdale and Ennerdale than the popular fells that plug the heads of these two valleys. Rising between the western end of each are a group of remote fells that are rarely visited and give a unique sense of wilderness seldom experienced in the Lake District. It is these quiet hills that form the basis of this walk, linking Wasdale with Ennerdale. Seatallan, Middle Fell, Haycock and Lank Rigg are the main summits visited. All rise above the magical 2000ft contour that allows them to be called mountains, rather than purely hills, and between them they cover some 30 to 40 square miles of terrain. The fells have smooth, rounded slopes that are cloaked in heather and are linked by rolling ridges.

DAY ONE

Starting from Wasdale Hall Youth Hostel, make your way to Greendale at the foot of Middle Fell, from where the fell walking begins. The south-west ridge of Middle Fell has a clear path that winds around small crags to reach the summit, with its large cairn of pinky-grey rock. Your efforts are rewarded by magnificent views across Wast Water to the Wasdale giants of Scafell, Great Gable, Kirk Fell and Scafell Pike.

The great heathery dome of Seatallan rises to the north-west and can be climbed from a broad hause just down the northern slope of Middle Fell. A faint path can be traced up its eastern flank, but soon you are left to find your own way across unpathed heather to the huge summit cairn and trig point. There are fine views which stretch from Scafell Pike to Black Combe – views which you can rest assured few other walkers will have seen as Seatallan is surely

the least visited of any of the Lakeland Fells.

Walk north from Seatallan over a depression before rising to the summit of Haycock, a delightful mountain which appears as a smooth cone when approached this way. To the north of the summit a fringe of crags tumble into Ennerdale, while slender ridges sweep both west and east and give easy access to neighbouring Scoat Fell, Steeple and Pillar.

The day is nearly over and you may be able to descend into Ennerdale with the sun setting over the lake to the west. The path follows the broad ridge that divides Deep Gill from Silvercove Beck leading to the head of Ennerdale Water.

DAY TWO

You get a chance to take a closer look at Ennerdale Water on day two as the route begins with a walk along its southern shoreline. A path leaves the lake shore after a stile, with a small beck on the left (named as Red Beck on the OS 1:25,000 map). A faint path traces the west bank of this beck through the

WALK FACTS

Start/Finish	Wast Water Youth Hostel, Wasdale Hall, GR 145045
Distance	Day one: 12.8km (8 miles)
	Day two: 19.3km (12 miles)
Total ascent	Day one: 1000m (3280ft)
	Day two: 600m (1968ft)
Time	Day one: 6 hours
	Day two: 7 hours

Difficulty A high-level fell walk over some rough and relatively remote terrain where paths can be difficult to trace. Good navigational skills required in low cloud
Accommodation The walk is based around the youth hostels at Wasdale Hall and Gillerthwaite, but there are also B&Bs and campsites nearby in both Ennerdale and Wasdale
Public transport Railway station at Seascale from where bus services run to Gosforth 8km (5 miles) away from Wasdale. Bus services run from Whitehaven to Kirkland and Ennerdale Bridge 11.5km (7 miles) from Ennerdale

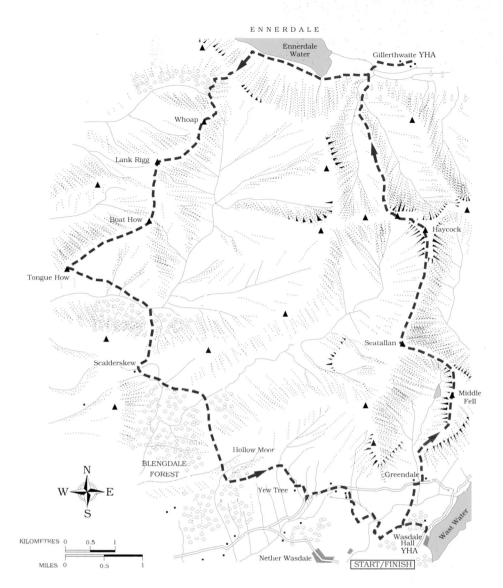

ENNERDALE

Ennerdale Water

Gillerthwaite YHA

Whoap

Lank Rigg

Boat How

Haycock

Tongue How

Seatallan

Scalderskew

Middle Fell

Greendale

Hollow Moor

BLENGDALE FOREST

Yew Tree

Wast Water

N W E S

Wasdale Hall YHA

KILOMETRES 0   0.5   1

MILES 0   0.5   1

Nether Wasdale

START/FINISH

ALONG THE WAY

Ennerdale is famous for the Dog of Ennerdale, which terrified the whole of the valley in 1810. After killing over 200 sheep, the dog was eventually shot by John Stel in Eskar Woods and his stuffed remains are exhibited in Keswick Museum. Ennerdale Water, formerly called Broadwater, has been a reservoir for around 130 years, serving the west coast's towns and industries. It is a glacial lake and its water is incredibly pure as there is little vegetation or wildlife living in it. It is very popular with fisherman as it has a good supply of trout.

Until 1989, Ennerdale had no electricity and there is still no public road through the valley, though in 1882 there was a plan to run a railway through the valley. Canon Rawsley and the Lake District Defence Society

opposed it fiercely and the *Pall Mann Gazette* published a 'Poetical Lamentation on the Insufficiency of Steam Locomotion in the Lake District'.

> *Wake, England, Wake! 'tis now the hour*
> *To sweep away this black disgrace –*
> *The want of locomotive power*
> *In so enjoyable a place.*
> *Nature has done her part, and why*
> *Is mightier man in his to fail?*
> *I want to hear the porter's cry,*
> *'Change here for Ennerdale!'*

The railway was abandoned but a number of battles have taken place over the years to bring motor traffic to the valley.

49

Below: Ennerdale from Crag Fell.
Bowness Knott on left

trees towards Whoap. While you ponder over the exact route of the path, as it is hard to trace, enlarging views over Ennerdale grow behind.

Finally the path breaks out of the trees and you have to make your way across rough pasture to a stile, leading to a broad track through the forest at the base of Whoap's northern slopes. Follow the stile and track through the forest to finally emerge at a stile and gate on the edge of the open fell, with Whoap clearly ahead. Navigation eases now as you walk south-east onto the shoulder of Whoap which leads easily to the first summit of the day. Grassy, pathless terrain takes you over a narrow neck linking Whoap with Lank Rigg, where you walk up a gentle incline over more unpathed fell to a little cairn, a trig point and a little tarn – the summit of Lank Rigg. The view is a worthy reward, although the close proximity of the Sellafield cooling towers may not be so welcomed.

From Lank Rigg easy walking south over rough grass takes you to Boat How, where you descend west over Tongue How to a bridleway. This is the first good path of the day and it will be welcomed, as by now you are no doubt growing tired of pathless moorland.

The bridleway takes you to Worm Gill which is crossed to enter Scalderskew Wood. Forest tracks continue to Scalderskew itself, from where the track continues east around the edge of the forest to cross the River Bleng and enter Blengdale Forest. A bridleway takes you through the trees in a south-easterly direction to emerge onto open fell for about 200m (655ft) before diving through another wood at Hollow Moor.

At the end of the Hollow Moor woods, you emerge onto a lane where you turn left and walk east alongside the woods. A series of bridleways, paths and roads take you to Yew Tree Farm, Gill, Buckbarrow Farm and finally Wast Water Youth Hostel.

A ROUND OF ESKDALE

The Lakeland backwater of Eskdale forms the basis for this two-day circuit which makes a complete circumnavigation of the valley. Eskdale is very sparsely populated, with only two small hamlets, Boot and Eskdale Green. There is also no lake of any size in the valley, which in itself may be the reason for the valley's lack of development. This walk encircles Eskdale using some ancient paths to find a sprinkling of tarns, farms and fell tops. Although the walk climbs the highest fells in the area none of these are very high, the highest point being on Green Crag at 488m (1601ft). The valley is broad and flat with the winding River Esk in its base. The lower altitude means that this walk will also provide views when the higher central fells are lost under a cloak of cloud and drizzle.

WALK FACTS

Start/Finish	Ravenglass, GR 085965
Distance	Day one: 14.5km (9 miles)
	Day two: 19.3km (12 miles)
Total ascent	Day one: 350m (1148ft)
	Day two: 500m (1640ft)
Time	Day one: 6 hours
	Day two: 7 hours

Difficulty A walk over low-level fells where paths are sometimes difficult to follow with some open moorland. Good navigational skills will be required
Accommodation B&Bs, campsites and hotels at Ravenglass and throughout the Eskdale valley, with a youth hostel in Eskdale
Public transport The Ravenglass and Eskdale Railway links the Eskdale valley with Ravenglass where there is a main line railway station with links to Lancaster and Carlisle. Irregular bus services link the towns and villages up the west coast

DAY ONE

The walk begins at the Irish Sea, in the seaside town of Ravenglass on the western seaboard of Cumbria. Muncaster Castle on the edge of Ravenglass is your first port of call, so leave the town by walking south, past Walls Castle, a former Roman bath-house to the ancient Roman fort, which has long since disappeared. A public right-of-way leads through the grounds of Muncaster Castle, the family home of the Penningtons since the twelfth century. The paths are clear through the wooded grounds and soon you are at the A595, from where Fell Lane leads onto Muncaster Fell through rhododendrons, birch and pine. The track was used by drovers when they took their herds of cattle and sheep to the Ravenglass markets. The track may have also been used by the Roman legions walking from Ravenglass to their fort at Hardknott.

Muncaster Fell provides a wonderful walk through bracken and heather, with views to Black Combe, Eskdale, Wasdale, Harter Fell and the Scafell massif as well as a view back over the shining sea and the Ravenglass dunes nature reserve. The fell is popular with those seeking a short afternoon stroll. The path finally descends to Eskdale Green railway station on the Ravenglass and Eskdale Railway. You must cross a road and walk a short distance to the right to pick up a path that leads over the railway and then go uphill in a north-north-easterly direction around the back of the Outward Bound Outdoor Centre. Finally you will emerge from the bracken at Siney Tarn, which is subdivided by invading rushes into separate tarns ringed by boggy marshland. Nearby, Blea Tarn is soon found nestling in a hollow of smooth crags.

With views of Eskdale ahead you are now drawn down through a bracken hillside to Beckfoot. Here you meet the railway once again and cross it to reach the main road through Eskdale. A lane on the right leads down to the banks of the River Esk and this provides an ideal way of reaching the Woolpack Inn and youth hostel further up the valley.

DAY TWO

The first day was quite easy going, but the second day is a little rougher as you now cross some wild untracked moors and take in some craggy mountain

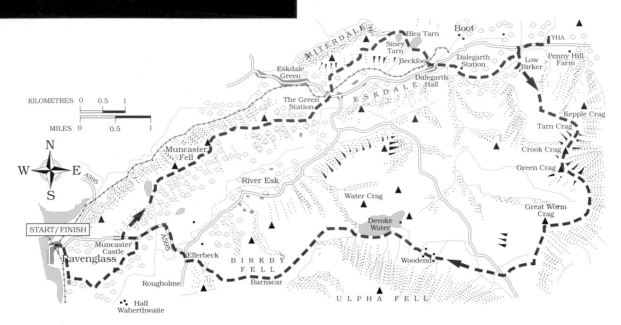

ALONG THE WAY

Ravenglass has been an important port over the centuries and when the Romans ruled over England it was the second largest port in the country. Its attraction was that it was the only naturally sheltered harbour on the west coast between the River Dee and the Solway Firth.

Today most people go to Ravenglass to visit 'La'al Ratty', the Eskdale and Ravenglass Railway that was originally built in 1875 to transport haematite from the iron mines in Boot to the main Furness railway line on the Cumbrian coast. When the last mines in Eskdale were closed in 1912 the railway should have been closed too but it was saved by Bassett Lowke, a model engineer, who converted the track to a more economical 15-inch gauge. The railway was nearly closed again in 1953, but this time it was Douglas Robinson of Muncaster who saved the line by buying it as a going concern. Today it is supported by the Wakefield family and many other supporters and it's very popular with tourists.

Muncaster Castle has been the family home of the Penningtons since the twelfth century. The family originally lived in the neighbouring bath-house until they moved into the pele-tower which was enlarged into a castle in 1325 and completely rebuilt as a mansion in about 1800. The fortifications were needed to provide protection against the Scots who had been raiding the area regularly since 1298, when William Wallace ravaged the northern counties as far south as Durham.

---

summits along the way. From the Woolpack Inn a track leads to Low Birker cottage and then up onto the fells. The walk as far as Tarn Crag is easy enough and your efforts are well rewarded with views to the Scafell and Bowfell massifs behind. But now the going gets tough as paths dissolve, leaving you to navigate your way carefully over Crook Crag and Green Crag, the highest point on the walk at 488m (1601ft). The view from this fell overshadows its altitude as it provides a stunning panorama to the north over Scafell, Bowfell and Crinkle Crags. To the east there's

an unusual view of the Coniston Fells and to the west the rolling wilds of the Ulpha and Birker Fells lead the eye to the shining Irish Sea. But perhaps most interestingly of all you can see almost all of the route followed during the two days.

Walk south from Green Crag, then west around a boggy hollow to Great Worm Crag, which marks the end of a broad grassy ridge. Ahead lies pathless wild moorland which you must cross in a south-westerly direction to meet the road linking Ulpha with Eskdale. Your next target is Devoke Water, the largest and highest lake in the Eskdale area. A road walk and track leads to Woodend, from where a bridleway continues across the fell and descends to the shore of Devoke Water. The tarn is famous for its red trout, which it is said were imported here from Italy by the abbots of Furness Abbey. But as with many parts of this walk it will be the stunning views to Scafell that will hold your attention.

To end the journey around Eskdale a bridleway is followed across the fells to Barnscar and Ellerbeck and finally the A595, from where it's a road walk to the grounds of Muncaster Castle and the end of the walk at Ravenglass.

Eskdale from Kepple Crag. Whin Rigg is the highest point on the right

BROUGHTON IN FURNESS TO ESKDALE

WALK FACTS

Start/Finish	Broughton in Furness, GR 212875
Distance	Day one: 16km (10 miles)
	Day two: 19.3km (12 miles)
Total ascent	Day one: 800m (2625ft)
	Day two: 1050m (3445ft)
Time	Day one: 6 hours
	Day two: 8 hours

Difficulty A walk over a rarely frequented area of small fells and moors where the paths are not always obvious and sometimes non-existent

Accommodation Youth hostels, camping and B&Bs in Eskdale, more limited selection of B&Bs around Broughton in Furness

Public transport Infrequent bus services extend to Broughton in Furness from the railway station at Foxfield. The Eskdale and Ravenglass Railway is the only public transport in Eskdale

The Duddon valley and Eskdale along with the rolling low-level fells that divide them, have much in common as they all remain virtually unspoilt and largely free of walkers and visitors for most of the year. The fells and moors in this part of the Lake District remain mostly unexplored and undeveloped. Perhaps it is the lack of glistening lakes and ribbons of foaming water descending over the crags that keeps the tourists away, or perhaps it is the lack of footpaths that mean you really need to know what you are doing if you are to find a route with map and compass alone. Whatever the reason, this forgotten corner of the Lake District offers a unique backpacking experience and backpacking is surely the finest mode of travel from which to view this barely tamed land.

DAY ONE

The main line railway station at Foxfield is well placed for the start at Broughton in Furness. A series of footpaths and lanes lead through Hagg and Hartley Ground to Pickthall Ground. Keep an eye on the map through these early stages and you'll soon be crossing the River Lickle, the source of which you'll cross at the end of day two when you traverse the rough hill ridge from White Pike to Caw. Pickthall Ground marks the start of the hill work, with footpaths leading up the southern slopes of Great Stickle and onto its trig point that marks the summit at just 305m (1000ft) above the sea that is so clearly in view to the south.

The rough fell of crags and tiny splashes of tarns provide interesting walking to Stickle Pike, with a wonderful first sighting of the River Duddon winding north-east into the heart of the Lake District. The quiet road can be used for your descent to the valley,

but there's also a bridleway descending west to Ulpha. Either route requires a bridge to cross the river and a short road walk to The Low, where a footpath climbs through woods and past old quarry workings to Brighouse and the edge of the moors of the Birker and Ulpha Fells.

The path hits the road known as the Ulpha Pass which leads directly across the moor to Eskdale. Brown Rigg marks the highest point of the road and from here you get clear views to Green Crag and Worm Crag, two nuggets of rock bursting from a carpet of heather moorland. There's no easy way to reach these wonderful rock forms and you have to head straight across the moor to Great Worm Crag and follow the broad ridge north-east to Wormshell How and finally to Green Crag. The summit brings views south over the Duddon and also west over the wild and largely untrodden moors.

A hint of a path here and there make the final stage easier as you walk over to Crook Crag, where you are confronted by a stunning panorama to the Scafell massif and Bowfell. This is often a particularly exciting moment for me, as so often I have enjoyed sunshine and fine weather on Crook Crag when the higher central fells are cloaked with cloud, mist and rain. How wonderful these outlying and low-lying fells are!

ALONG THE WAY

Broughton comes from the Old English name Brocton, meaning a farmstead or hamlet beside a river. The 'in-Furness' was added to distinguish this place from several other Broughtons in the area. The village has a spacious market place grouped around an obelisk, erected to celebrate the Golden Jubilee of George III in 1810. Broughton market was a collecting place for wool and coppice wood products in the eighteenth century, the cargo being taken by barge out of the Duddon estuary. Today the market is held on a Tuesday, when livestock fills the town.

The Duddon Valley is delightful walking country and much less visited than much of Lakeland. Wordsworth explored the valley during his

Stanley Force

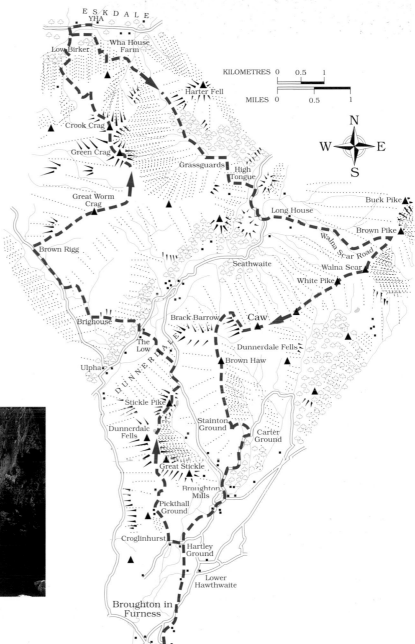

childhood and described the River Duddon as his 'favourite river' and later, in 1820, wrote *The River Duddon: A Series of Sonnets* in which he described the wildness and beauty of the river throughout its length in a series of thirty-four sonnets.

The Walna Scar Road is an ancient route that links Coniston with the Duddon Valley and was in the past maintained to allow horse-drawn traffic. It has been used to carry slate from the neighbouring areas and in 1954 a local youth took the first-ever photograph of a flying saucer here! The Walna Scar Road can be naturally linked to the Grassguards Pass between the Duddon Valley and Eskdale and no doubt in the past this whole route would have been used for the carriage of trade by teams of packhorses as well as for moving livestock to the Ravenglass market.

An obvious path takes you north from Crook Crag and down into Eskdale via Low Birker and Doctor's Bridge to arrive on the road near the Woolpack Inn with a youth hostel and campsite nearby.

DAY TWO

You depart the Eskdale valley by following the lane opposite the Woolpack Inn through Penny Hill Farm and towards the valley that passes under the western slopes of Harter Fell. The path is a bridleway and is used by mountain bikers making the traverse from Coniston to Eskdale by way of the Walna Scar Road. The track rises to a col and then begins to descend into the Duddon Valley by following the edge of the plantation through Grassguards to High Tongue.

Among the woods, a bridge takes you over the River Duddon which has started life high up on Wrynose Pass to the north-east. Once again careful map reading is required as you pick your way through the lanes and footpaths of the Duddon valley, which lead over Tarn Beck, a minor tributary, and past Long House to join the Walna Scar Road. Although called a road, this is really just a rough track, although on occasions drivers of four-wheel-

Dunnerdale viewed over Ulpha to Hesk Fell on the right and Pike Side on the left

drive vehicles have done battle with the road and forged a way across the fells.

The Walna Scar Road climbs up to Walna Scar Fell, with splendid views over the Duddon Valley, to Harter Fell rising like a pyramid from the forests that adorn its lower slopes. At the height of the pass, you leave the well-trodden ways and begin a crossing of wild, rough fell. White Pike marks the end of the main ridge, with its cairn and fine panorama to the north that consists of the Scafell and Bowfell ranges.

A soggy hollow marks the start of the climb up to Caw, a hill that is set among disused quarry workings. Walk north from Caw to pick your way past the crags and down to an old mine level leading to Brack Barrow and Brown Haw. Once again you have to leave the easiest path and clamber up rough fell to Brown Haw's summit. More rough fell leads south to the end of the ridge and then you descend to a clearer track and Carter Ground. A final series of lanes and field paths return you to Broughton in Furness.

BORROWDALE TO WASDALE

It was with good reason that the early pioneers came to the head of Borrowdale and Wasdale to discover what the Lakeland mountains really had to offer and set the sport of rock climbing alive with tales of adventurous forays onto the highest mountains in England. For between these two valleys rise a map maker's nightmare and a walker's dream, with contours that twist and fold at every turn. One moment you can be standing on smooth pasture, the next scrambling up sheer rock faces. But this is not only a place for rock gymnasts, for the rock that makes fine crags for climbing also makes fine mountains for walking and here the backpacker could wander for days and still not have seen every crease or wrinkle in this spectacular mountain landscape.

DAY ONE

You begin with a road walk to the Mountain View Cottage at the foot of Glaramara, from where a path leads through a coppice of holly and rowan into the mouth of the valley that spawns Combe Gill. The path climbs over Thornythwaite Fell and on to the summit of Glaramara, with its wonderful views to Great Gable and down the length of Borrowdale. Glaramara is separated from Scafell Pike by Esk Hause, where a stone wind-break acts as a popular meeting point for seasoned walkers who know that this small stone cross is the last shelter of any size before stepping onto England's highest fell.

A line of cairns leads the way onto the shoulder of the Scafell massif, but it is Scafell Pike's satellite, Great End, that draws the attention. This huge, sleeping giant has one of the finest north-facing cliffs in the Lake District and every winter climbers come from all over England to test their skill on its early grasp of snow and ice. From the top of Great End you can peer down one of the classic ice climbing routes, Central Gully, a long narrow rift extending top to toe of the north cliffs.

Returning back to the main path you are led south-west over the pavement of tilted slabs and boulders between Broad Crag and Ill Crag, another two fine satellite peaks of the Scafell massif. Here, time spent drifting around is never wasted, as every turn brings a refreshing view down Upper Eskdale or to Great Gable.

A steep drop into the head of Little Narrowcove signals the start of the final haul onto Scafell Pike's summit. But once again the best views come to those who walk untethered from the summit trig point. Scafell and Scafell Pike may have similar names and similar locations, but they stand completely isolated from one another, almost like two separate mountains. The great divide is formed by a huge cliff that makes walking between the summits virtually impossible. There are scrambles and climbs up these cliffs, of course, but the walker and backpacker must use a more intricate and far from obvious method of reaching the top. You begin from the head of

WALK FACTS

Start/Finish	Seatoller, GR 245137
Distance	Day one: 16km (10 miles)
	Day two: 12km (7.5 miles)
Total ascent	Day one: 1500m (4922ft)
	Day two: 1100m (3609ft)
Time	Day one: 7 hours
	Day two: 6 hours

Difficulty A walk on clear paths over England's highest mountains, on mostly rocky terrain and clear, high-level mountain paths

Accommodation Youth hostels, campsites and B&Bs in Wasdale and the Seatoller area of Borrowdale

Public transport Regular bus services link Seathwaite at the head of Borrowdale with Keswick and the railway station at Penrith. There is no public transport down Wasdale

Opposite: Hiker on Great End above Esk Hause

ALONG THE WAY

Seathwaite at the head of Borrowdale has the distinction, according to the records, of being the wettest inhabited place in England, with over 300cm (120in) of rain a year, while Esk Hause gains the title of wettest in England due to its 380cm (150in) of annual rainfall which reached 455cm (180in) in 1928. But this is an extreme micro-climate, for only 9.5km (6 miles) away at Grange the rainfall is two-thirds of Seathwaite, while at Keswick it is less than half. At **Wasdale Head** there is a tiny church. On the south window one of the small leaded shapes contains a stained glass Napes Needle (the name of a spire of rock on Great Gable) with a biblical quotation: 'I will lift up mine eyes unto the hills from whence cometh my strength'.

The window is a memorial to those members of the Fell & Rock Climbing Club who lost their lives in World War I.

One of the farmers who lived at Wasdale Head during the first half of the nineteenth century was Will Ritson, who kept a small inn as a sideline (now the Wasdale Head Inn). There are mementos to his days as the biggest liar in Cumberland at the inn.

Mickledore and then descend south-east to follow the Foxes Tarn path all the way back up and over the 900m contour to the summit of Scafell. There are fine views over all Lakeland from Scafell and many would agree that it is by far the finer viewpoint of the mighty duo. The descent to Wasdale is via the Burnmoor Tarn path, where you turn right to reach the valley floor at Wasdale Head.

DAY TWO

The second leg of this walk begins by entering the valley of Mosedale and climbing to the Black Sail Pass. At the crest, Kirk Fell rises abruptly to your right. There is no clear avenue of weakness, but if the path is followed it will find its way by weaving a course up a rocky cleft onto Kirk Fell's broad multi-summited plateau. The higher summit is marked with a wind-break and an iron fence post. Cross the summit and descend easily to Beck Head and its tarn, with the north-west ridge of Great Gable waiting ahead.

The climb to Great Gable is obvious but it's rocky

and hard going on tired limbs. When the end is near you have to scramble over huge boulders to reach the rocky plateau, guided by cairns to the summit outcrop. There's a Fell & Rock Club Memorial plaque on the summit, which remembers seventeen members of the club who lost their lives in World War I. The best views are gained by walking 100m (328ft) from the summit towards Wasdale Head. Here the Westmorland Cairn marks the finest view in the Lake District, according to the two brothers who built the cairn in 1876; and with the patchwork pastures of Wasdale Head carpeting the valley floor below your boots and Wast Water leading the eye to the coast, who could disagree?

You leave Great Gable by turning your back on the view of Wasdale and heading for Borrowdale. The path is clear and leads down into Windy Gap before clambering over Green Gable, where a view of Ennerdale will force you to stop for a while, before tracing the path north into Gillercombe and down the banks of Sourmilk Gill to Seathwaite, a short walk from Seatoller.

BORROWDALE TO ESKDALE

The far-flung corner of Eskdale is possibly the most inaccessible valley in the Lake District, a haven of rough rock and quiet solitude and a wild place by Lakeland standards. But with Scafell and Scafell Pike on its doorstep, Eskdale has much to offer those who are in search of remote trails. Many regard the Eskdale approaches to the Scafell massif as the finest routes of the mountain. The routes are long, remote and give a welcome break from the popular trails. In Eskdale the walker can feel a sense of wilderness, as you walk beside the winding River Esk, hunt paths over barren slopes and look for a dry way around a soggy bog. This route makes a traverse between Borrowdale and Eskdale, taking in the Scafell massif en route as well as neighbouring Bowfell and Esk Pike.

DAY ONE

A clear path leaves the road opposite Mountain View cottages and takes you onto Thornythwaite Fell and finally onto the twin summits of Glaramara. I'm never really sure which is the highest of these, although the north-eastern top marks the finest view that extends down the length of Borrowdale but also to the flat table top of Great Gable. Nevertheless, I always clamber onto the second summit too, just to be sure that I have truly reached the top!

A path takes you south now across the rough fell to the rocky turret of Allen Crags, with a clear view down to the crossroad of paths at Esk Hause – the Spaghetti Junction of mountain paths with paths radiating to Allen Crags, Langdale, Esk Pike, Upper Eskdale, Scafell Pike, Sty Head, Langstrath and

WALK FACTS

Start/Finish	Seatoller, GR 245137
Distance	Day one: 17.7km (11 miles)
	Day two: 16km (10 miles)
Total ascent	Day one: 1250m (4101ft)
	Day two: 1200m (3937ft)
Time	Day one: 8 hours
	Day two: 7 hours

Difficulty High-level fell walking on clear paths over England's highest mountains. Much of the terrain is rocky and serious in foul weather when navigation could be difficult

Accommodation Youth hostels, B&B, hotels and camping around Seatoller at the head of Borrowdale and in the Eskdale valley

Public transport Regular bus services link Seathwaite at the head of Borrowdale with Keswick and the railway station at Penrith. The Ravenglass and Eskdale railway serves Eskdale from Ravenglass railway station

Grains Gill. Our route tackles Esk Hause the tenth highest peak in the Lake District. Esk Pike wasn't named on OS maps until the mid-1960s. Prior to this time it was only recorded as a spot height of 885m (2903ft), but then Esk Pike has always been a secondary peak which is climbed en route to somewhere more exciting such as Scafell or Bowfell. Despite this Esk Pike provides a fine, grandstand view of Scafell Pike rising boldly above Upper Eskdale.

Bowfell is reached by crossing Ore Gap and then making the long haul to the summit, which is marked with a huge cairn, which also stands on the old Cumberland and Westmorland boundary. Bowfell rises at the head of three valleys, Eskdale, Langdale and Langstrath, so not surprisingly the views are some of the finest in Lakeland.

A steep, rough path takes you to Three Tarns which lies between the slopes of Crinkle Crags and Bowfell. This is where you leave the clear trails and dive down a cairned path to the banks of Lingcove Beck, one of those forgotten corners of the Lake District where few walkers wander. A climb onto Hard Knott and Border End brings views to Scafell Pike and down the length of Eskdale and this is surely enough to make this diversion worthwhile. But you

ALONG THE WAY

Bowfell's summit is regarded by most people as the finest viewpoint in the Lake District, but the mountain is also famous for the rumour that it sends the magnetic needle of a compass spinning on its axis. This is said to occur near Ore Gap, where the well-trodden path exposes a red sub-soil, indicating the presence of a vein of haematite iron ore, hence the name Ore Gap and the effect on the magnetic compass needle. I've never had the problem and some say it only occurs when a compass is placed directly on a rock, so clearly this shouldn't affect your navigation too much.

The **Hardknott Roman Fort** at Eskdale has been described as one of the most spectacular forts in Europe. It stands at a half way point on the Roman road between the forts at Ambleside and Ravenglass and it was used to police the road over Hardknott Pass. Today, clear remains can be seen of the flat parade ground, the barrack blocks, the bath-house and store rooms.

When the poet Samuel Taylor Coleridge arrived on the summit of **Scafell** in 1802, he was faced with the problem of getting down. From Scafell he spotted 'A ridge of Hill' [Mickledore] joining Scafell to Scafell Pike, describing the feature like a 'hyphen between two words'. But then Coleridge fell into the trap of attempting to descend directly to this ridge, over the steep cliffs. The route he followed is known as Broad Stand and is given the grade of three by scramblers. Coleridge was lucky to have survived the descent, but this marked the completion of the first recorded ascent and descent of Scafell.

are now also well placed to visit Hardknott Fort, one of the best-preserved examples of a Roman fort in England. With your accommodation in Eskdale only a short road walk away, it's worth spending a little time here to appreciate what it must have been like to have been a Roman soldier in this wild corner of the Lake District.

DAY TWO

The return to Borrowdale from Eskdale takes you over the highest mountain in England and getting to the top requires a long haul, so it's wise to set off early. The path leaves the roadside opposite Wha House Farm in Eskdale, near the youth hostel and takes you up to Slight Side, the outlying top of Scafell. Slight Side is a real turning point in the walk, as it's the end of the rough moorland and the start of the rocky, craggy terrain that has made Scafell one of the finest rock climbing arenas in the UK.

The summit of Scafell brings views across Scafell Pike, the highest mountain in England, but it has to be said that from this angle Scafell Pike appears lower and slightly below your feet. This was the conclusion

Sunset from Scafell Pike

of the pioneers too and why Scafell Pike was so named as it was thought to be only a 'pike' or satellite peak of Scafell.

Getting to Scafell Pike from Scafell is far from obvious too. Vertical cliffs bar a direct approach and the easiest route follows the Foxes Tarn path from the summit, which leads down the south-eastern flank of the mountain to emerge below the cliffs. A steep scamper up scree leads to Mickledore and then easier walking continues to Scafell Pike.

Clear paths lead from Scafell Pike over the rocky plateau to Esk Hause. A short diversion away from the path to climb Great End brings stunning views to Glaramara and down the length of Borrowdale to distant Derwent Water and Skiddaw. The final leg of the journey leads north-west from Esk Hause, under Great End's towering cliffs and past Sprinkling Tarn to Sty Head and Styhead Tarn. This is a popular route and there's no difficulty in following the path down the banks of Styhead Gill to Seathwaite and finally Seatoller in Borrowdale.

LAKELAND'S 3000ft MOUNTAINS

Of all the mountain challenges that exist, the Lakeland 3000ers is one of the finest mountain marathons in England. The marathon trek is often tackled by fell runners who complete the route in a day. But it is also a popular challenge for fit walkers who can take it a little easier and aim for a two-day round during the height of summer when the extra hours of daylight make the challenge slightly easier.

There are four mountains that rise above the 3000ft contour in the Lake District – the highest point in England, Scafell Pike 977m (3205ft), Scafell 964m (3163ft), Skiddaw 931m (3054ft) and Helvellyn 950m (3117ft). To climb them all is to traverse the roof of England.

WALK FACTS

Start/Finish Keswick, GR 265235
Distance Day one: 42km (26 miles)
Day two: 42km (26 miles)
Total ascent Day one: 1464m (4803ft)
Day two: 1680m (5512ft)
Time Day one: 14 hours
Day two: 14 hours
Difficulty A very long trek on clear paths. To complete this you will need to be very fit, travel very light and treat the walk as a marathon challenge, rather than a walk. To make life a little easier deposit your overnight luggage in Grasmere.
Accommodation Youth hostels, B&Bs, hotels and campsites at Grasmere and Keswick
Public transport Regular bus services link Keswick and Grasmere with the railway stations at Windermere and Penrith

Mickledore and Scafell from Scafell Pike

DAY ONE

Everyone who tackles the 3000ers begins from the Moot Hall in Keswick. From here it's a dash down Lake Road into Borrowdale. A lakeside path takes you to Friar's Crag, with views down Derwent Water to the Jaws of Borrowdale. As there isn't much time and plenty of miles to pack in, the walk sticks to the shore-line path around Derwent Water but you have to walk along the road to Grange. Here you can cross the bridge over the River Derwent and trace a riverside path through the woods of Borrowdale to Longthwaite Youth Hostel. Stay with this path as it continues through woods and across fields to finally emerge at Seatoller. More road walking leads down to Seathwaite. At last the fells are within striking distance and a clear path up to Sty Head deposits you among the highest fells in England.

Leave Sty Head by taking the Corridor Route under Great End to cross the head of Piers Gill and emerge at Lingmell Col, between Lingmell and Scafell Pike. A clear path leads to Scafell Pike. This is the highest point in England, but it is only our first 3000er with still three more to climb!

Scafell is your next target, but things start to get tricky now as the towering crags of Scafell bar any easy access. There are a number of options available. One way is to tackle Lord's Rake, which follows a roller coaster path under Scafell Crag that emerges onto the smooth slopes above the cliffs. The rake contains loose rock and earth and can't be recommended, but it is a way to the top. Another alternative is Broad Stand, which is a grade three scramble that tackles Scafell's east buttress directly via a narrow gap in the rock below Mickledore. You'll

Opposite: Skiddaw from Latrigg

ALONG THE WAY

Skiddaw was thought to be the highest mountain in England until the 1820s. The remoteness of the Scafell massif meant that it was not generally recognised as being of any particular significance. But local opinion in West Cumberland thought it knew better and in 1779 William Wilberforce recorded being shown, 'a high hill with a kind of crack in it … said by local people thereabouts to be higher than Skiddaw'. This was **Scafell**.

The **Moot Hall** in Keswick is now home to the tourist information office but it has been the traditional starting point for challenge events every since Bob Graham ran around 42 Lakeland peaks in 23 hours 39 minutes on 13 June 1932. The man was 42 at the time, hence the number of peaks, and his time for the event has dictated that a round of under 24 hours was the target to beat. To this day young and old hopefuls take on the challenge of the Bob Graham Round at the height of summer.

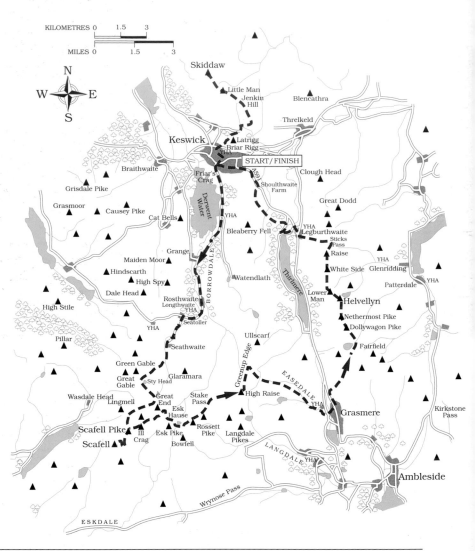

need plenty of experience and skill before tackling this, but for those with that experience this is the most direct means of climbing to Scafell.

Most walkers should turn to the Foxes Tarn route. This approaches Scafell from the Eskdale side of Mickledore. A path climbs up through Scafell's east buttress, passing a tiny tarn *en route*. It then climbs up to the summit of Scafell on a clear path. You can take a short rest on the summit but not too long as there is still a long way to go.

A descent back down the Foxes Tarn path is the

best way to return to Scafell Pike. You then need to head for Grasmere to find your overnight accommodation. The most direct line is to follow the main path over Broad Crag, Ill Crag and Great End to Esk Hause, with its stone wind-break providing an opportunity for a short break. From here you can follow the path to Angle Tarn, before turning east to Stake Pass on a smaller track. A long unpathed slog then awaits as you drag yourself up from Stake Pass to High Raise. This is a great place to take another breather as you are standing in the centre of the Lake

District, with your next targets Helvellyn and Skiddaw clearly in view.

Descend towards Greenup Edge and then turn right to follow the clear path down into Easedale. You'll no doubt want to save your energy so stick with the valley route that leads directly into Grasmere without a single hill to climb.

DAY TWO

The second half of the walk begins with a punishing haul up to Grisedale Tarn. The path leaves the main A591 road just to the north of Grasmere and skirts Tongue Beck throughout its climb to Grisedale Tarn. To add insult to injury you must then tackle the steep zigzags that lead up to Dollywagon Pike. By now you'll be feeling pretty tired, but thankfully the going eases a little as you make the long high level traverse of the Helvellyn massif.

The walk follows a broad path which eventually rises to the summit of Helvellyn without any difficulty. A large stone wind-break provides a welcome shelter as you take in the view that includes Scafell, Scafell Pike and Skiddaw, which still awaits the attention of your boots.

Leave Helvellyn by walking to Lower Man, White Side and Raise before descending via Sticks Pass to Legburthwaite above Thirlmere. The low level journey to Keswick continues by crossing the A591 and taking the paths that lead alongside the woods to Shoulthwaite Farm. But you must eventually rejoin the A591 road and follow it down into Keswick.

Skiddaw is the last remaining 3000er of the round. The ascent begins from the north side of the town, so stay on the A591 road as it passes around the town following the river. Just after the park, turn right down Station Road past the youth hostel and over the River Greta. Follow the road as it swings to the right and then left under the disused railway bridge to arrive at Briar Rigg. A path leads from here around the slopes of Latrigg to a car park. The tourist route up Skiddaw begins from here and leads up over Jenkin Hill and Little Man to the summit.

Skiddaw marks the end of the walk, in many ways. All that remains is to take in the view to Scafell, Scafell Pike and Helvellyn, which can all be seen from Skiddaw. Finally return by the route of ascent back to Keswick.

THIRLMERE SKYLINE

This walk makes a complete circumnavigation of the fells that overlook Thirlmere lake, which marks the divide between the Central Fells and the Eastern Fells. It lies in a natural divide which stretches through Grasmere and Rydal to Windermere. The geological fault was eroded by water and enlarged by the retreat of ice; originally Thirlmere was narrow enough to be bridged. But now the lake has been dammed and the water level raised to provide a water supply to Manchester. The lake is enclosed by a dark green tide-mark of trees and is bordered by a busy road linking Grasmere to Keswick. This road was originally used as a main route for the wool trade, but in the eighteenth century it was used as a primary route by which tourists discovered the Lake District.

WALK FACTS

Start/Finish	Grasmere, GR 338075
Distance	Day one: 24km (15 miles)
	Day two: 17km (10.5 miles)
Total ascent	Day one: 810m (2657ft)
	Day two: 920m (3018ft)
Time	Day one: 7½ hours
	Day two: 6 hours

Difficulty High-level fell walking on clear paths. The first section is very boggy after rain, but day two is over drier, rockier terrain

Accommodation B&Bs, campsites, hotels and youth hostels at Grasmere and around the northern head of Thirlmere

Public transport Regular bus services link Keswick and Grasmere with the railway station at Windermere

Walking south on Helvellyn towards Nethermost Pike

ALONG THE WAY

Dunmail Raise at the southern end of Thirlmere has always been a focal point as it marks the watershed between Morecambe Bay and the Solway Firth, the divide between southern and northern Lakeland and the boundary between the old counties of Westmorland and Cumberland. A pile of stones between the lanes of the dual carriageway are said to cover the remains of the last king of Cumberland. The battle was fought on Dunmail Raise in 945 between King Edmund of England and King Dunmail of Cumbria. Tradition says that King Dunmail died in the battle; however, other records show that the king lived for another thirty years, finally dying on a pilgrimage to Rome. It appears strange then that the pass was named after him.

The road between **Grasmere** and **Keswick** has changed little since it was improved in the late eighteenth century, although the flooding of Thirlmere by the Manchester Water Authority in the 1880s raised the level of the water by around 15m (50ft) and forced a new road to be built. The old one is now under water.

Sticks Pass is an old trade route linking Thirlmere with Ullswater and was first used regularly when the mines around Glenridding became important in the Elizabethan era. The route over the pass was originally marked out with sticks, hence the name. The sticks have long gone but the path is clear enough these days.

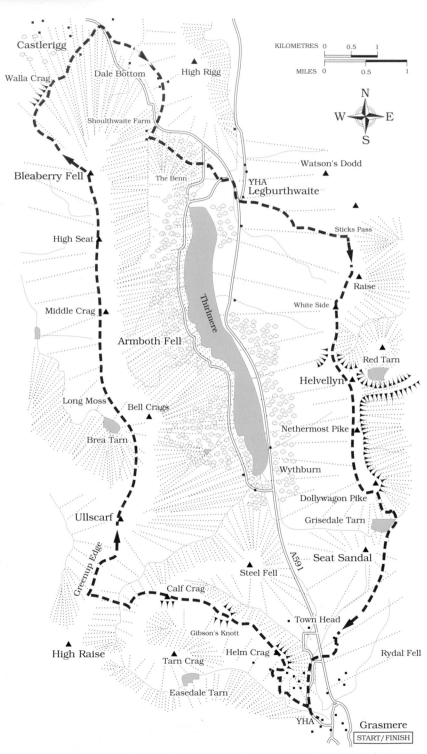

DAY ONE

You begin the walk from Grasmere by heading down Easedale Road past Goody Bridge to a small cluster of buildings under Helm Crag. A rough track leads through these buildings to the base of the fell, from where the hill climbing begins onto the crag. This is a steep climb, with views over Grasmere and the Easedale valley to take in as you huff and puff.

Finally you arrive at a plateau, with Fairfield rising gloriously across the valley to the east. A short climb carries you onto to the summit ridge of Helm Crag, which is one of the most difficult fells to truly get to the top of as it is a steep scramble. Even Wainwright didn't climb to the top of this one!

A lofty walk over grassy mounds and rocky plinths carries you along the ridge with views to the Coniston and Langdale Fells to the west. To the east, Fairfield, Grisedale Hause and Dollywagon Pike form an unmistakable skyline. At Far Easedale you turn to the right to cross the head of Wythburn before clambering up to Greenup Edge. In mist, many people have walked down Wythburn by mistake, so take care with your navigation unless you fancy a very short walk indeed!

The traverse to Bleaberry Fell is renowned for being soggy after rain, so pack your gaiters and wear them before it's too late. There's a steady pull to Ullscarf, from where some fence posts guide you to Standing Crag. A popular bridleway linking Thirlmere with Wythburn crosses the ridge here, but stick with the high ground over Shivery Knott, Middle Crag and High Tove. This is the high point of the walk today as it is relatively dry and provides a fine panorama in all directions so it is the best place to take a lunch break.

Bleaberry Fell is the last summit of the day, with excellent views to Skiddaw and Blencathra to the north. The final leg is to descend to Walla Crag in a north-westerly direction and then walk along the top of the crags to Rakefoot Farm, with campsites close by. If you continue through Rakefoot Farm and follow a path through fields to the A591 there are more campsites at Dale Bottom and Bridge End Farm, with a youth hostel nearby at the entrance to St John's in the Vale.

View south over Thirlmere from near Raven Crag with Helvellyn on the left

DAY TWO

Today it will mighty Helvellyn that comes underfoot as you make your way back to Grasmere by way of Thirlmere's eastern skyline. The climb begins from Legburthwaite near the youth hostel where a path traces Stanah Gill to Sticks Pass. At the crest of the climb, leave Sticks Pass in a southerly direction for Raise. The views from here are superb, but this is a fell that is bypassed by many walkers who concentrate their efforts on the popular neighbouring peaks.

The walking is easy now and a line of cairns lead south-west to White Side, with the fine cone of Catstycam rising beyond Keppel Cove throughout the walk. A descent leads to a long stony ridge, with views down into Brown Cove on the left and Brown Cove Crags on the right. The ridge culminates on Lower Man. There's a great view back along the route covered so far, which is worth more than a backward glance.

You now join the path that has risen from Thirlmere via Helvellyn Gill. This is the most

Approaching Helvellyn's summit shelter

popular route on Helvellyn and it leads easily to the nearby summit. There's a trig point and more importantly a four-sided stone wind-break on the summit. But the best views are available away from the summit, so keep walking to find a quiet spot, perhaps overlooking the rim of Nethermost Cove, a short distance to the south, with its views to Striding Edge.

A lofty walk along the escarpment continues south around Nethermost Cove to Nethermost Pike. The main path traverses the hills some way down the slope to the west, but for views into the marvellous eastern combes stick to the edge of those cliffs. At Dollywagon Pike the main path avoids the summit, but again a diversion is worth the effort for the views down the length of Grisedale, with St Sunday Crag rising like a great whale to the east. A steep, knee-jerking descent down zigzags leads to Grisedale Tarn from where a clear path descends down the bank of Tongue Gill to Grasmere.

LANGDALE TO ESKDALE

Eskdale seen from Border End. Harter Fell and Hardknott Pass road are on the left

The tremendous mountain barrier of Crinkle Crags, Bowfell, Esk Pike and the Scafell massif, separates the valleys of Langdale and Eskdale. These are fine goals for any walk, but it's the valleys linked by this walk that are of particular interest, as although they have a common boundary, that is where the similarity ends. Langdale is the popular centre of walking in southern Lakeland and for many people it is a natural yearly pilgrimage, where the only intention is to scale the infamous Langdale Pikes that are well worn by footpaths with plenty of other walkers to follow should you lose your way. Conversely Eskdale is wild and remote by Lakeland standards, with no easy route of access, little public transport, few farms, few pubs and very few other people to follow. This makes Eskdale a far more serious mountain experience where navigational skill, mountaincraft and self-reliance are regularly required.

DAY ONE

To sample a little of Eskdale and experience the difference between the two valleys, this walk begins in Langdale, where clear paths and a trace of walkers can be followed onto the high fells. As with so many walks in Langdale, this one begins from the Old Dungeon Ghyll Hotel where many walkers have spent the day drying off next to the fire after a wet day on the 'Pikes'.

The path through Mickleden carries you under the great climbing cliffs of Raven Crag and Gimmer Crag and on towards the banks of Rossett Gill. A steep zigzagging track squeezes you between the slopes of Bowfell and the Rossett Gill ravine. The final haul is tough by anyone's standards, with your feet slipping on the scree and loose rocks. But when you emerge and take a well-earned breather you are greeted with that classic view down Langdale, its U-shaped form so much a textbook example of how a glaciated valley should look.

A path leads around the lip of Angle Tarn's cradle to Esk Hause, where a large, stone wind-break provides valuable protection against the elements on this exposed mountain path junction. If you stay on the main path you'll end up in Borrowdale or Wasdale, so pause for a moment and check your map for the route that winds around the southern flank of Great End and onto the Scafell massif.

WALK FACTS

Start/Finish	Langdale, GR 287061
Distance	Day one: 16km (10 miles)
	Day two: 16km (10 miles)
Total ascent	Day one: 1050m (3445ft)
	Day two: 900m (2953ft)
Time	Day one: 7 hours
	Day two: 7 hours

Difficulty High-level fell walking on clear paths over the highest fells in England. Much of the terrain is rocky and serious in foul weather when navigation could be difficult, but there are a wide variety of escape routes

Accommodation Youth hostels, campsites and B&Bs in Langdale, Elterwater and Eskdale

Public transport Regular bus services link Langdale with Ambleside and the railway station at Windermere

Opposite: Bowfell seen at sunset from Pike o' Blisco

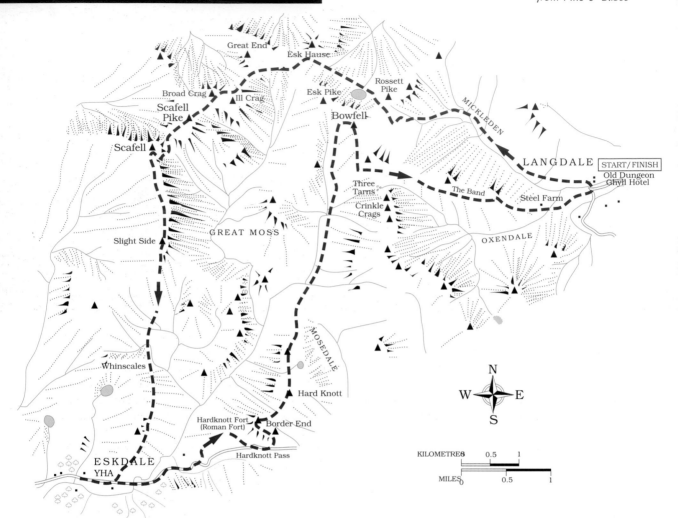

ALONG THE WAY

Eskdale means the valley of the River Esk, the river that rises at Esk Hause, the highest foot pass in Lakeland at 759m (2490ft) above sea-level. The water then flows through Great Moss, a soggy hollow surrounded by an amphitheatre of towering mountains including Scafell, Scafell Pike, Esk Pike, Bowfell and Crinkle Crags. The river continues through Upper Eskdale where it is squeezed through rocky gorges before finally emerging into the Eskdale valley itself.

The Eskdale valley has no lakes and only a sprinkling of tiny tarns but it is a beautiful valley with a rich variety of landscape – from the rocky crags of its mountains to the green meadows and woodlands of its plains. It lies remote and wild with just a scattering of farms and cottages lining its 21km (13 miles) course to Ravenglass on the coast of Cumbria.

The **Roman fort** at **Hardknott** was built in AD130 to guard the road that linked the Roman forts at Ambleside and Ravenglass, which was a busy port. The fort was built by Emperor Hadrian and an inscription to prove this was found outside one of the gates of the fort and is now in Carlisle museum. It has been suggested that after some time the fort was left to a caretaker and the bath-house used as an inn for travellers between Ravenglass and Ambleside.

The route becomes more rocky now as you climb over the roof of England. You will have to boulder hop to negotiate the rocky outlying summits of Ill Crag and Broad Crag, from where particularly impressive views extend across Great Moss and Upper Eskdale. The climbing ends with a steep final pull onto Scafell Pike, where a huge cairn, a trig point, a panoramic view and plenty of wind breaks let you know that you've reached the top of all England at 977m (3205ft) above sea-level.

The easiest route between Scafell Pike and Scafell descends south-east down scree from Mickledore. A small break in the cliffs gives access to the Foxes Tarn route that leads almost directly to the summit of Scafell. The long descent into Eskdale now begins and you can really feel yourself slipping into a quieter, more relaxed world as you walk south-east over Slight Side and then south to the road in Eskdale.

DAY TWO

Eskdale is so quiet that you won't see many cars on the road and there'll be few if any walkers to follow as you begin your road walk up Hardknott Pass. You can leave the road, towards the start of the steep climb, to wander through the remains of Hardknott Roman Fort, which is said to be the finest example in Britain if not Europe. It's interesting to walk around the remains of the walls and to march across the large flat parade ground but to really appreciate the fort, you can't beat an aerial view. So continue through the remains, join the road to the top of Hardknott Pass and then climb onto Hard Knott and Border End. The views from here over the Roman fort to the long sweep of Eskdale are outstanding. All the shades of green colour the patchwork floor of the valley with the River Esk winding through woods to the distant coastline of Cumbria. Your efforts are also rewarded with views to Scafell and Scafell Pike.

An undulating traverse continues across Border End with views to Bowfell and Esk Pike ahead. You descend into the valley to find Lingcove Beck, which is followed north towards Ore Gap, between Esk Pike and Bowfell. Near the source of Lingcove Beck is your last chance to look back at quiet Eskdale for the secluded feel of the walk changes suddenly at Ore Gap as you meet a large path linking Esk Pike to the left with Bowfell to the right. Turn right to Bowfell, with its summit marked by a huge cairn and outstanding views across the whole of the Lake District and as far as the Pennines. But it is quiet, remote and wild Eskdale that will hold your attention and stay in your mind as you return to Langdale by way of The Band and treat yourself to a well-earned drink in the Old Dungeon Ghyll Hotel.

CONISTON TO LANGDALE

You can't really say you know a place until you've climbed its mountains, travelled the length of its valleys and investigated every twist and turn of its landscape. So in search of a wider appreciation of the Langdale and Coniston area, this walk not only climbs over its highest fells, but also wanders around the valleys. It links the village of Coniston with the Langdale valley, taking in parts of the Cumbria Way through Tarn Hows and Langdale before tackling the high fells of Pike o' Blisco, Swirl How, the Old Man of Coniston and Dow Crag.

At the end of the two-day journey you will have climbed high fells where the views

WALK FACTS

Start/Finish	Coniston, GR 301975
Distance	Day one: 14.5km (9 miles)
	Day two: 19.3km (12 miles)
Total ascent	Day one: 200m (656ft)
	Day two: 650m (2132ft)
Time	Day one: 5 hours
	Day two: 7 hours

Difficulty A mixed route of high-level fell walking and low-level valley walking, but with clear paths throughout

Accommodation Youth hostels, campsites, hotels and B&Bs at Coniston and Langdale

Public transport Regular bus services link Coniston and Langdale with Ambleside and the railway station at Windermere

extend to the distant coastline of Cumbria as well as to the mighty central fells. But you will have also experienced the villages, woods and lanes of Cumbria, areas that can offer as much intrigue as the high fells but are so often ignored and unappreciated by mountaineers and mountain walkers.

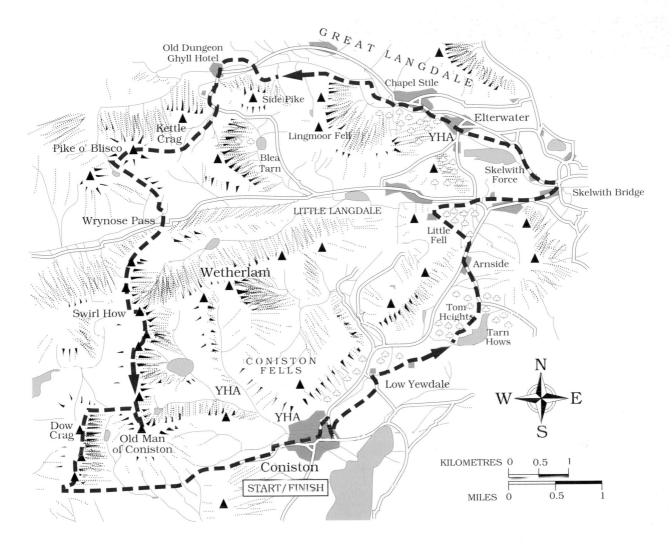

Left: Elterwater village with Wetherlam under snow behind

ALONG THE WAY

Tarn Hows is a delightfully irregular miniature lake surrounded by wooded fells and sprinkled with a scattering of islands. It is certainly one of the most beautiful places in the Lake District and is very popular, but, surprisingly, it is an artificial lake. The beauty spot is named after a nearby farm and was originally a swampy tarn known as Monk Coniston Tarn. Around the end of the nineteenth century the local landowner built a dam to create one large tarn with two principal islands. The surrounding area was then planted with larch, spruce and pine, which look particularly beautiful against the backdrop of Wetherlam and the brooding high fells. Strictly speaking Tarn Hows refers to the surrounding fells of the lake, as 'how' means hill and 'tarn' means lake.

Elterwater is an old Norse name meaning 'lake of the swans' and even today it is often visited by whooper swans. The lake also attracts herons, coots, moorhens, mallards, tufted duck, grebes, mergansers and mute swans among its reedy banks. The neighbouring village to the lake is also called Elterwater and its small cluster of cottages are mainly built from local green slate, which gives the village a very attractive appearance.

DAY ONE

Wetherlam and the Old Man of Coniston dominate the skyline of Coniston village but turn your back on these towering peaks for a moment and instead head for the Cumbria Way, a long-distance path that links Ulverston to Carlisle by following a route through the valleys of the Lake District.

The Cumbria Way leaves Coniston by crossing a stone bridge over Yewdale Beck, opposite the village school. The path leads up through woods and along the banks of the beck before emerging onto a lane. You can turn left here to pick up a path on the right after about 100m. This leads into Tarn Hows Wood, past Tarn Hows Cottage and finally to Tarn Hows itself, with its lake and beautiful wooded surroundings. This is one of the most photographed places in the Lake District and is popular with tourists. Tarn Hows isn't completely natural though as there were originally three small pools, where today one large lake exists. It was created in the nineteenth century as a beauty spot. Although the Cumbria way

follows the main track, it is also possible to pick out a path that climbs Tom Heights, to the west of the lake, which provides views to both Wetherlam and the Langdale Fells. You can then rejoin the main route near Arnside.

You meet the A593 road at Arnside, but this is short-lived as you only have to turn right onto a footpath which runs parallel with the road and then left onto a track heading north-west under Little Fell for High Park Farm. This path takes you through Tongue Intake Plantation to Park Farm and on to Skelwith Bridge. There's a coffee shop in the Kirkstone Slate Gift shop, if you fancy a drink and a sticky cake, which you surely will by now.

The Cumbria Way continues into Great Langdale along the bank of the River Brathay to Elterwater and Elterwater village. There's a youth hostel and some B&Bs here, if you fancy a short day. But you could keep walking along the river bank to find a campsite opposite the Old Dungeon Ghyll Hotel or stay in the O.D.G. itself at the head of Langdale.

Above: The view to Wetherlam from the summit of Pike o' Blisco. Below left: The Old Man of Coniston as seen from the ridge to the south

DAY TWO

Day one has been quite easy on the legs, but this is more than made up for on day two, which takes a high-level route, starting with Pike o' Blisco. To begin with you have to tackle more tarmac, past Wall End Farm and up the steep zigzags towards Blea Tarn. You'll see a clear path on the right leading to Pike o' Blisco and this is your route. The path is rough underfoot but it gets you to the top where your efforts are well rewarded with views to Bowfell and Wetherlam. There's a steep descent to Red Tarn, but then an easier path takes you away from the Langdale Fells towards the Coniston Fells.

At Wrynose Pass you'll find the Three Shires Stone which marks the old boundary of Cumberland, Westmorland and Lancashire. Cross the road over Wrynose Pass and climb a narrow path up onto Wet Side Edge, with views down the length of Wrynose Bottom to your right throughout the climb. Although

this is steep to begin with, the angle soon eases, with Swirl How coming underfoot easily. Although not the highest of the Coniston fells, Swirl How is surely the finest viewpoint, particularly with the cairn perched so close to the cliffs that tumble into Greenburn, with the view extending over Little Langdale and beyond. It's an easy stroll along the top of the cliffs to the Old Man of Coniston, with views over the cliffs to Levers Water and Low Water, two tarns that nestle beneath the eastern escarpment of the ridge. The summit of the Old Man of Coniston is a fine place to watch a sunset, as it rises high above all of its surroundings providing views to the west coast of Cumbria. There are, however, more shapely summits where this route leads next, such as Dow Crag.

A path leads north-west to Goat's Hause, the col at the head of Goat's Water, and then you climb up and over Dow Crag, with its superb cliff scenery and airy views down to Goat's Water. The view to the north over the Scafell range of fells is particularly impressive. By following the long south ridge of Dow Crag you will reach the Walna Scar Road, which can be followed all the way back to Coniston village.

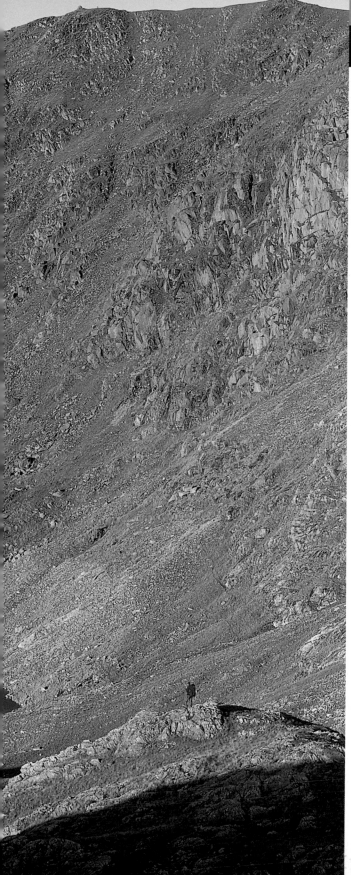

CONISTON TO ESKDALE

The high fells above Coniston are linked with the quiet valley of Eskdale in this two-day walk. There is much variety in the scenery as day one takes in the high fells of the Coniston range, while day two follows part of a low-level route along the old trade route between Ravenglass and Coniston. Goods would have been carried on pack ponies while livestock would have been herded along the route, both eventually arriving at the market of the ancient port of Ravenglass. Throughout the journey you rub boots with disused mine workings, Roman forts and packhorse bridges, while views to the Scafell massif, the central fells and the lower south-western corner of Lakeland, are never far from sight.

WALK FACTS

Start/Finish Coniston, GR 301975
Distance Day one: 14.5km (9 miles)
Day two: 16km (10 miles)
Total ascent Day one: 1142m (3746ft)
Day two: 551m (1807ft)
Time Day one: 6 hours
Day two: 5 hours
Difficulty A high-level fell walk on day one, with some sections on untraceable paths. Lower level route on day two
Accommodation Youth hostel, campsites, B&B and hotels in Coniston and Eskdale
Public transport Regular bus services link Coniston with Ambleside and the railway station at Windermere. The only public transport in Eskdale is the Ravenglass and Eskdale Railway which extends from Ravenglass to Dalegarth Station. Ravenglass has connections to the west coast main line

Previous page: Looking over Low Water at sunrise to the Old Man of Coniston

ALONG THE WAY

In almost every valley of the Lake District there has been some form of mining activity since Roman times and this has always provided valuable work not only for the miners themselves but also for the local craftsmen whose skills were required to service the industry. But perhaps the most obvious mine workings are those around the **Coniston Coppermines** valley. The area is rich in copper and iron ore, while large numbers of coppiced woods have also been used to make charcoal. The copper mines were opened in the fifteenth century, but they were considerably developed in the nineteenth century, when slate quarrying also began. This hive of industry led to the Furness Railway between Foxfield on the coast and Coniston being opened in 1859 to transport the materials which had previously been moved by boat along Coniston Water or by pack ponies over the mountains. When the mines became unprofitable they had to be closed and the railway was taken up too. Today all that remains are the mine levels, some rusting machinery and a scattering of former mine buildings. The Coniston Coppermines Youth Hostel exists in the converted mine manager's office. The whole Coppermines area provides a fine opportunity to discover the industrial heritage of Coniston. But a note of warning: there are still mine shafts in the valley and these are definitely *not* safe to explore and are best avoided.

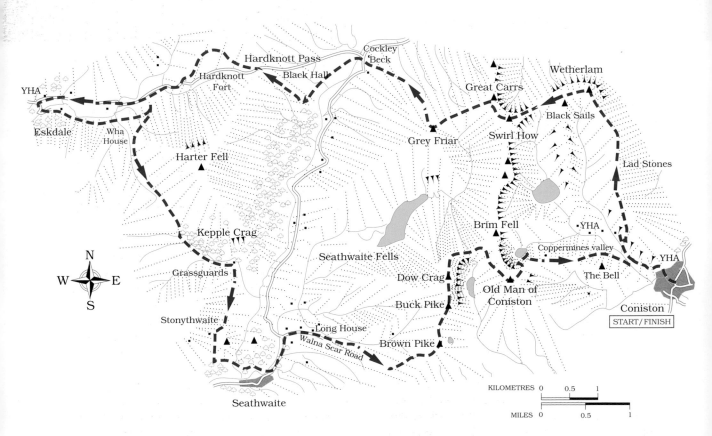

DAY ONE

Wetherlam is the first peak of the day, so head for the Coppermines valley from Coniston. There are a number of routes that can be taken from the village, but the easiest is probably to follow the signs to the Sun Hotel. A sign beside the hotel directs you to 'Old Man and Levers Water' and over Church Beck, with the track continuing into the Coppermines valley. Here the remains of the mine workings are clearly evident, with scraps of iron scattered among the spoil heaps. Even though the remains of the workings aren't a pretty sight, it has to be remembered that they are part of the Lake District story, these mines at one time providing extensive employment for the people of Coniston.

A path on the right climbs up behind some cottages to Hole Rake and over to Tilberthwaite. Follow this path to its highest point and then leave it for a track that is less distinct but is heading the right way, which is north over Above Beck Fells. The ridge is broad and a path becomes easier to trace as height is gained. You walk close to the cliffs of Lad Stones, with views east to Windermere, finally reaching the sprawling summit of Wetherlam, with its spectacular views to the north, east and south.

The Old Man of Coniston seen from the summit of Swirl How with Dow Crag to the right

Easy walking takes you around the skyline towards Swirl How with views to Langdale and Little Langdale away to the right. The walk around the head of Greenburn is spectacular with vistas sweeping down the whole length of the valley to Little Langdale. Along the way you'll pass the remains of an aircraft undercarriage that crashed on these fells at the end of World War II.

It's time to leave the obvious trail and strike out south-west for the rounded crest of Grey Friar. There are twin cairns on the summit, with the one nearest to the Old Man of Coniston being slightly higher. There is a good view from here to Harter Fell and across Wrynose Bottom to the mighty central fells.

You have to find your own way down the fellside to Wrynose Bottom, as although a path is marked on the map none seems to exist on the ground. Once you reach the valley floor you join the route taken by Roman legions who would have marched over Wrynose Pass and Hardknott Pass between their forts at Ambleside and Eskdale. From the roadside at Cockley Beck, a Roman road leads to Black Hall from

Below: Walking the ridge to Swirl How from the Old Man of Coniston

where a path climbs up the side of the plantation to the summit of Hardknott Pass. The nearby Hardknott Roman fort was built between AD117 and 138 to hold a garrison of 500 men. The Roman soldiers no doubt greeted their arrival at the fort with its bath-house with great relief after their 16km (10 mile) march from Ambleside. For the modern traveller accommodation in Eskdale is only a short walk down the road.

DAY TWO

You return to Coniston by way of an ancient trade route that would have been used by pack ponies and drovers. A lane opposite the Woolpack Inn leads to the first packhorse bridge, called Doctor's Bridge, which was named after Dr Edward Tyson who had the bridge widened in 1724. The track leads through Penny Hill Farm on the south bank of the River Esk and up to the open fell below Kepple Crag and Dow Crag. The path joins a larger track to provide an easy walk down to Grassguards. Stepping stones take you over the River Duddon, but you'll need the map to find your way around the base of High Tongue to Tarn Beck and the lane near Long House. But things become easier again as this lane climbs up to join the Walna Scar Road which can be followed all the way to Coniston.

The views build behind to Scafell and Scafell Pike as you reach the highest point on the Walna Scar Road. The walking has been fairly easy, so if you have the energy why not end the day with a round of Brown Pike and Dow Crag? A steady descent around the head of the valley leads to Goat's Hause and the climb up to the summit of the Old Man of Coniston. A final series of leg-punishing zigzags takes you past Low Water, through the remains of the mine workings and back to Coniston.

DERWENT WATER SKYLINE

Resting in beautiful Borrowdale, arguably England's finest valley, Derwent Water has been called the 'Jewel of the Lakes', the 'Queen of the Lakes', the 'Elysium of the North' and it is generally regarded as the scenic climax of the Lake District. But you don't get a lush green landscape and a full lake without plenty of water so a shower or two over Borrowdale isn't unusual, indeed the valley claims the record for the highest rainfall in England! In poor weather some Victorian travellers described Derwent Water as the Devil's chamber pot, due to the dank and misty weather that so often brews from the Jaws of Borrowdale at the southern end of Derwent Water. Surrounding Derwent Water there's a fine series of hills, including the wonderful Cat Bells, High Spy and Dale Head ridge to the west. To the east, Bleaberry Fell and High Seat form the watershed between Derwent Water and Thirlmere.

DAY ONE

Keswick is the capital of northern Lakeland and it is the natural starting point for this walk as the shore of Derwent Water is easily reached from the centre of town. To get to the hills you have to walk along the B5289 towards Portinscale. This road takes you over the River Derwent and here you can follow a footpath along the banks of the river to Portinscale and through the woods at Fawe Park. The path continues through Overside Wood before finally reaching the foot of Cat Bells.

That's the end of the low-level walking for a superb ridge walk awaits your attention. Cat Bells is a popular fell but with views over Derwent Water, Keswick and

WALK FACTS

Start/Finish	Keswick, GR 265235
Distance	Day one: 16km (10 miles)
	Day two: 16km (10 miles)
Total ascent	Day one: 937m (3074ft)
	Day two: 550m (1805ft)
Time	Day one: 5½ hours
	Day two: 5 hours

Difficulty A high-level fell walk on clear paths, with a very boggy section from Watendlath to Keswick
Accommodation B&Bs, campsites, hotels and youth hostels at Keswick and around the head of Borrowdale around Seatoller and Longthwaite
Public transport Regular bus services link Keswick with railway stations at Penrith and Windermere. There's also a bus service from Keswick to Seatoller

the whole of Borrowdale, is this any surprise? The lake can be seen stretching some 6.5km (4 miles) down the valley with High Seat and the Helvellyn range easily identified across the water to the east.

Wonderful high-level ridge walking continues over Maiden Moor and then on to High Spy. There are some spectacular cliffs here which sweep down into the head of the Newlands valley. If you look carefully you'll spot disused mine workings, where copper, lead and smaller quantities of gold and silver were mined from the Elizabethan times to the beginning of the nineteenth century. Tunnels penetrate deep into the Newlands fells but they were all eventually abandoned due to the costs of working at such distances from the surface.

From High Spy you descend to a small col before climbing steeply to Dale Head, with its proud summit cairn and particularly fine view down the Newlands valley to Skiddaw. It's downhill now as you head into Borrowdale by leaving Dale Head in a southerly direction to reach the summit of the Honister Pass, the watershed between Borrowdale and Buttermere. Green slate has been mined here since the seventeenth century and although the underground mines are now closed, mining still continues on the surface of the surrounding fells. A roadside path, which was originally the route of a toll road, can be traced down to Seatoller where there's a campsite. Alternatively head for Longthwaite Youth Hostel, the campsites near Stonethwaite or the various B&Bs in the area.

ALONG THE WAY

Derwent Water means the 'lake of the river which abounds in oak trees'. The name 'Derwent' is fairly common through British river names with examples that come from the same root name including the River Darent in Kent, the River Dart in Devon, the River Darwen in Lancashire and the River Derwent in Derbyshire and Yorkshire.

Derwent Water receives water from all the surrounding fells, with water making its way into the lake from the Thirlmere watershed to the east and the Cat Bells ridge to the west. More water makes its way into Derwent Water from the hills at the head of Borrowdale, including Great Gable, Glaramara and the Esk Hause watershed, this being funnelled down the River Derwent into Borrowdale, Derwent Water and then Bassenthwaite from where it makes its final journey into the Irish Sea.

The whole area of **Watendlath**, including the tarn and the beautiful stone packhorse bridge, is owned and protected by the National Trust. More interestingly Watendlath didn't receive mains electricity until 1978 and was the last hamlet in the Lake District to be connected. There are still many single buildings scattered about the fells that rely on a private generator for their power supply, such as the youth hostel at Honister Pass.

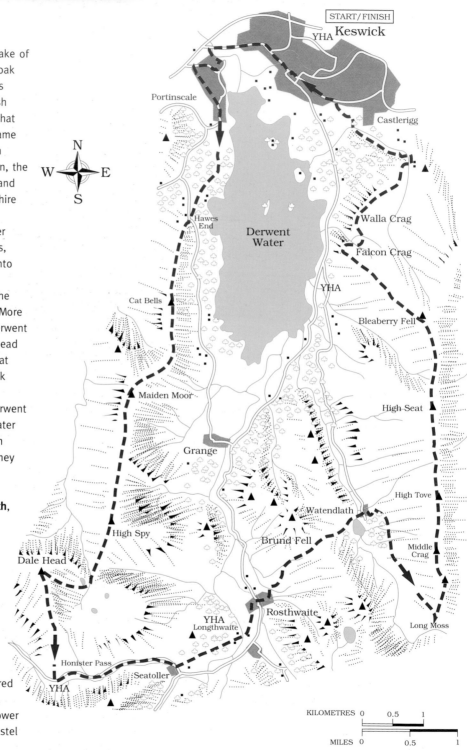

DAY TWO

The second half of the journey around Derwent Water kicks off with a stiff climb from Rosthwaite over to Watendlath. You begin by crossing the bridge over Stonethwaite Beck in Rosthwaite, and follow the path to the left as it climbs up to its highest point at Puddingstone Bank. Here you get superb views back over Borrowdale, with Seatoller, Rosthwaite and Stonethwaite nestling at the hub of a broad patchwork of green meadows and scattered farmsteads. Beyond them rise the soaring crags of Glaramara and the distant fells of Dale Head and Fleetwith Pike.

Descending from Puddingstone Bank you soon arrive at the small hamlet of Watendlath, with its small tarn, stream and stone packhorse bridge. Among the tiny cluster of whitewashed farm buildings, weary walkers may get some refreshments or a bite to eat from the café. This wonderful place is hidden from the outside world as it sits in a secluded fold in the fells, with only a long, narrow, winding stretch of tarmac providing access for road-users.

Leave Watendlath on the path which climbs south-east to Long Moss and Blea Tarn, the

Derwent Water and the Newlands Fells; Cat Bells, Causey Pike and Grisedale Pike

watershed that separates Thirlmere from Derwent Water. From Blea Tarn you turn north to follow an old fence line along the watershed over Middle Crag to High Tove. This section will be tough going any time of year other than a very dry spell, so pack gaiters for your legs and be prepared to wear them. But to make up for the soggy going underfoot the view to the west is excellent from here and includes Scafell Pike and Great Gable, while Helvellyn is the principal point of interest to the east. Surprisingly no lakes are in view even though Derwent Water and Thirlmere are so near.

The traverse ends on Bleaberry Fell, from where you descend north-west to Falcon Crag, one of the finest viewpoints available of Derwent Water and a favourite haunt of landscape photographers and day trippers. A clear path leads around the top of the Walla Crag cliffs with stunning views across Derwent Water at all times. An easy walk continues to the road end at Rakefoot and down to the outskirts of Keswick.

LANGDALE SKYLINE

The Great Langdale valley is possibly the most popular valley in the Lake District and the reason is simple: it is surrounded by superb fell walking. The hills have a similar character to those of Coniston, Wasdale and Eskdale, which are all far more difficult to get to than Langdale. The valley was scraped into a classic U-shape by a glacier that slipped out of the valley, clawing an intricate maze of hanging valleys, cliffs, gills and tarns. The shaping of the land has given modern walkers a wealth of classic walks over the Langdale Pikes, Bowfell and Crinkle Crags, while Pike o' Blisco provides stunning views across the valley. Lingmoor Fell provides a less strenuous outing though a justifiably popular route around the fringe of the valley. The broad rolling ridge from Silver How to Blea Rigg is more often walked from Grasmere, but in this walk it serves to provide an interesting contrast to the shapely hills of the Great Langdale valley.

DAY ONE

The little village of Elterwater stands at the gateway to the Great Langdale valley, thus providing the natural starting point for this walk around the valley's skyline. The day begins with a road walk towards Grasmere up Red Bank, but you can leave the tarmac near the top of the zigzags where a path cuts across the open fell to Dow Bank. Spedding Crag and Silver How come underfoot with ease, but there are plenty of paths that could send you the wrong way so keep an eye on the map. Things improve when you reach a couple of tarns beneath Lang How. The largest of these is home to a colony of black-headed gulls which take flight upon your arrival turning the sky into an umbrella of feathers.

WALK FACTS

Start/Finish	Elterwater, GR 328047
Distance	Day one:16km (10 miles)
	Day two: 17.7km (11 miles)
Total ascent	Day one: 850m (2789ft)
	Day two: 1400m (4593ft)
Time	Day one: 6 hours
	Day two: 7 hours

Difficulty A high-level fell walk with many clear paths and plenty of opportunities to escape into the valley
Accommodation Youth hostel and B&Bs at Elterwater, B&Bs, hotel and campsite at head of Langdale
Public transport Regular bus services link Elterwater and the Old Dungeon Ghyll Hotel in Langdale, Ambleside and the railway station at Windermere

At Blea Rigg there are a number of cairns and everyone seems to disagree over which is the highest, so put your hand on all of them to be sure of hitting the summit. The Langdale Pikes are now clearly in view with Pavey Ark being your first objective. Stay on the highest ground as far as Sergeant Man, then make your way to Thunacar Knott, with its summit cairn sitting among a mess of boulders. You are now ideally placed for the 'Pikes', with Pavey Ark's spectacular summit coming easily underfoot. The view over the cliff to Stickle Tarn and down the length of the Great Langdale valley is stunning.

Cairns lead around the Stickle Tarn basin to Harrison Stickle, which again offers fine views from its rocky crown. Many walkers leave Harrison Stickle and head directly for the dome of Pike o' Stickle, but a finer tramp is to descend across the head of Dungeon Gill and then climb to Loft Crag, for the view from here down Langdale is not to be missed. If you now continue toward Pike o' Stickle you are rewarded with views over Gimmer Crag, a superb piece of rock that is popular with rock climbers.

Pike o' Stickle is a strange knob of rock and you'll need your hands to get to the top, but the view is wonderful and you'll realise how rounded the summit is when you stand on it! A steady walk over Mart Crag Moor to Stake Pass provides easy access to the valley floor to end the first stage of the walk at the Langdale campsite or the Old Dungeon Ghyll Hotel.

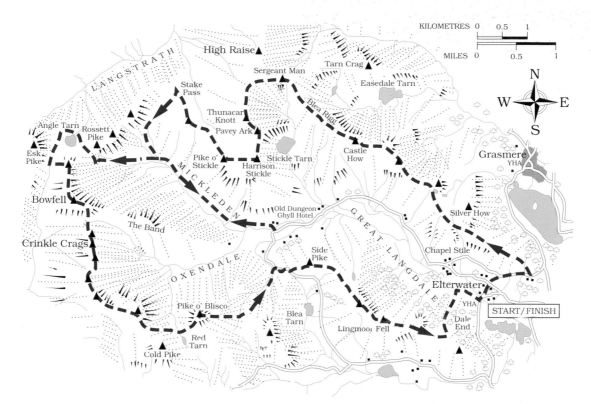

ALONG THE WAY

The **Great Langdale Valley** is a huge and beautiful glaciated valley with a broad, flat floor ringed by rock turrets that rise like cathedral spires, completely dominating the views. Wordsworth pronounced of Great Langdale that it: 'should on no account be missed by him who has a true enjoyment of grand separate forms composing a sublime unity...'.

Pavey Ark, one of the Langdale Pikes, has a great 152m (500ft) high cliff and this is by far the most striking rock formation in the valley. It is climbed by rock gymnasts with ropes and 'sticky' boots, but mere walkers have to seek alternative routes to the top. There are three routes onto Pavey Ark. An easy path for walkers is described in this route that tackles the summit from the northern slopes, although as the Lakeland guidebook writer Alfred Wainwright noted in his pictorial guides, 'Easy Gully on Pavey Ark is far from easy and Jack's Rake is downright difficult'. But of all the challenges in the Lake District Jack's Rake is one of those routes that fell walkers feel obliged to attempt sooner (but preferably later) in their fell-walking careers. It tackles a right to left rising traverse of the Pavey Ark cliff and is graded as one in the scrambling guides. But with a rucksack for a two-day walk, tired limbs and a lot of walking ahead of you, it is perhaps wise to avoid such antics until later in your walking career.

Bowfell with The Band descending to the Langdale Valley

Below: Hikers at the southern end of Crinkle Crags. Bowfell is the pointed summit in the distance

DAY TWO

You need to get yourself back onto the high fells at the start of day two, so walk back down Mickleden and follow the zigzags up Rossett Gill to Angle Tarn. Ore Gap is close by and this gives access to the long pull onto Bowfell. The largest cairn of all is retained for the summit crown of Bowfell, along with, arguably, the finest views available, although I must confess I've spent more days in cloud on Bowfell than anywhere in the Lake District!

Although Crinkle Crags looks like a narrow ridge from the valley, you'll now realise that they are a broad, rocky mass punctuated by deep ravines with a clear track across the top. But as always in the mountains, you get the best views if you leave the paths to peer over the edge of the cliffs and gullies. The highlight of Crinkle Crags is the Bad Step, a famous rocky cleft that only takes a couple of moves but may be tricky with a big rucksack and is an often-quoted talking point in the O.D.G. (Old Dungeon Ghyll) hotel bar. Thankfully you can avoid this by leaving the summit of Long Top on a path that follows cairns to the right to emerge below the Bad Step.

A long downhill leads past Great Knott to Red Tarn. But every downhill demands an uphill in the Lake District, so as soon as you reach the shore of Red Tarn you have to clamber uphill, this time to Pike o' Blisco. The mountain is almost conical, matching the walkers' dream mountain, and your efforts are rewarded with views to Bowfell, the Langdale Pikes and Wetherlam.

Once again this roller-coaster route sends you downhill, this time to the road under Side Pike. A path climbs Side Pike and a wall guides you along the crest of Lingmoor Fell. The path continues in a south-easterly direction and then begins to descend past old quarries to a lane near Dale End. Turn left here and follow the lane to Elterwater.

GRASMERE TO ULLSWATER

Wainwright's famous Coast-to-Coast walk links St Bees Head on the west coast with Robin Hood's Bay on the east coast. During the 200-mile journey walkers are confronted with superb scenery and a choice of routes. Between Grasmere and Ullswater, for example, walkers have a choice between pitting their skills against Helvellyn and Striding Edge or the steady slopes of St Sunday Crag, 'a mountain for connoisseurs' according to Wainwright. This walk tackles both of these options in a two-day circuit that links Grasmere with Glenridding.

ALONG THE WAY

Patterdale lies in magnificent surroundings of high fells and a lovely lake and is truly Alpine in nature. Still unspoilt, it is blessed with a character that is unique to the Lake District. Little has changed over the years with no cheap tourist attractions to beckon sightseers. Visitors here are attracted by the walking and mountaineering on the neighbouring fells.

Striding Edge is a narrow ridge that provides airy views and its dangers are more apparent than real. However, the ridge does sometimes claim lives and the Gough Memorial commemorates a man who was killed after a fall from the ridge in 1805. His faithful dog guarded the body for three months before it was found.

Grasmere village nestles in a bowl of fells beside a lake of the same name. It is home to Lakeland's most famous sporting event, the Grasmere Sports, William Wordsworth's grave and Dove Cottage where he lived for many years.

St Sunday Crag is the alternative route to Striding Edge that many Coast-to-Coast hikers follow on their journey between Grasmere and Patterdale. This requires far less effort than Striding Edge and provides a classic view of Ullswater. But it also gives splendid views to Fairfield and across the great gulf of Grisedale to the Helvellyn Range.

WALK FACTS

Start/Finish	Grasmere, GR 337076
Distance	Day one: 12km (7.5 miles)
	Day two: 14km (8.7 miles)
Total ascent	Day one: 750m (2460ft)
	Day two: 830m (2723ft)
Time	Day one: 5 hours
	Day two: 6 hours

Difficulty Straightforward walking on clear paths over high fells. The traverse of Striding Edge is narrow, requiring the use of hands at one point. Alternative route down Grisedale valley can be used to avoid Striding Edge

Accommodation Campsites, B&Bs and youth hostels at Grasmere and Glenridding

Public transport Regular bus services between Grasmere and the railway station at Windermere. Less frequent bus services link Glenridding with the railway station at Penrith

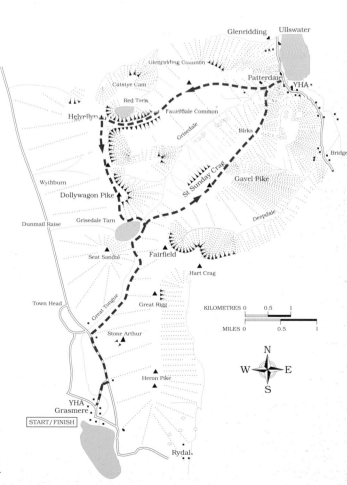

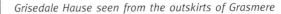
Grisedale Hause seen from the outskirts of Grasmere

DAY ONE

You could begin the walk at Grasmere or Ullswater but as public transport is far more regular to Grasmere, this is where this description begins. Leave Grasmere for the A591 road and take the track opposite Mill Bridge that leads around Great Tongue towards Grisedale Tarn. There is a choice of routes. The easiest way is to follow the path on the right, up the banks of Tongue Gill. But if you prefer a more challenging climb followed by a steady traverse then stay left, to climb up the north-western flank of Great Tongue. Both routes culminate in a gust of wind from the east as you reach the shoreline of Grisedale Tarn. The steep slopes of Dollywagon Pike lie across the water and it is down these slopes that you will return. The main route continues to St Sunday Crag via Deepdale Hause. But if the weather is not in your favour you could simply descend into Grisedale. The path is clear leading directly to the shore of Ullswater.

To reach Deepdale Hause, follow a path from the north-eastern end of Grisedale Tarn. This crosses a soggy hollow and then climbs steadily up to Deepdale Hause. Your efforts are matched by ever-expanding views down Grisedale and across the northern escarpments of Dollywagon Pike, Nethermost Pike and distant Helvellyn. The final pull to the summit of St Sunday Crag is along a broad ridge with a clear path. From the top the view to Fairfield is particularly impressive, while the view north to Dollywagon Pike, Nethermost Pike and Helvellyn is dominated by Lakeland's most famous ridge, Striding Edge.

The journey into the valley from St Sunday Crag is all downhill. On the way you are greeted with views of Ullswater, the lake forming a giant arc below a skyline of rugged fells. The tiny houses, hotels and hostelries of Patterdale seem like a model village at first, but soon come to life as you cross a stile and join a road. Turn right here to Grisedale Bridge and then take a left to Glenridding.

DAY TWO

Today you climb Striding Edge to Helvellyn and then traverse the skyline over Nethermost Pike and Dollywagon Pike to the now familiar shore of

Griesdale Tarn. The traverse of Striding Edge is one of the airiest walks in this book, demanding the use of hands to negotiate a steep step. Lovers of narrow, lofty ridges will enjoy the exposure, the views beneath the feet and the adventure. But if this is not your idea of fun, then take the low-level alternative up Grisedale valley, rejoining the outward journey at Grisedale Tarn. A lane from Grisedale Bridge leads into the valley from where a clear path traces Grisedale Beck to its tarn.

Those heading for Striding Edge should walk down the lane from Grisedale Bridge, beside Grisedale Beck. Then cross the beck and head up the flank of Birkhouse Moor towards the ridge. Striding Edge truly begins from Hole-in-the-Wall, where walkers often take a break before proceeding with the traverse. As you progress along Striding Edge the ridge becomes narrower. A line along the crest is the purist's way, but in winds or if you simply don't like that sort of thing, then you should follow a path along the northern flank.

The relatively easy progress is disturbed by a deep cleft below the summit of Helvellyn, known as the

Dollywagon Pike (left) and Helvellyn (middle distance) from Deepdale Hause

Bad Step. A couple of steps and it's over, although some people will make those steps last a lifetime. It's then just a short steep plod to the summit of Helvellyn. An aircraft landed here in 1926 and there's a monument to the event. You may also spot the Gough Memorial and Dixon Memorial along the way, which all add to the Helvellyn saga.

Helvellyn marks the end of airy ridge walking and the beginning of a high level stroll along a rolling plateau. Views, views and more views are the hallmark of this section, which gently descends from the 950m (3117ft) summit of Helvellyn to Nethermost Pike and Dollywagon Pike. The path bypasses the summit, but a short deviation is worth the effort for the stunning view to St Sunday Crag and down Grisedale.

Steep zigzags lead from Dollywagon Pike to Grisedale Tarn. The return to Grasmere retraces the outward journey along the path beside Tongue Gill and Great Tongue.

HIGH STREET AND HELVELLYN FROM AMBLESIDE

A walk around the classic Fairfield Horseshoe from Ambleside provides stunning views, particularly to the High Street and Helvellyn ranges. But having reached the summit on a one-day outing you are forced to beat a retreat before nightfall. This two-day walk covers some of the best sections of the Fairfield Horseshoe but also takes in many of the landmarks seen from Fairfield, including Red Screes, Striding Edge, Helvellyn and High Street. During the return leg it makes a traverse of Striding Edge and Helvellyn. Finally the route leads back to the summit of Fairfield, where you can drink in the view before descending to Ambleside.

WALK FACTS

Start/Finish Ambleside, GR 375044
Distance Day one: 19km (12 miles)
Day two: 19km (12 miles)
Total ascent Day one: 1400m (4593ft)
Day two: 1500m (4922ft)
Time Day one: 8 hours
Day two: 8 hours
Difficulty Straightforward walking on clear paths over high fells. The traverse of Striding Edge is narrow requiring the use of hands at one point. Alternative route down Grisedale valley can be used to avoid Striding Edge
Accommodation Campsites, B&Bs and youth hostels in Ambleside, Patterdale and Glenridding
Public transport Regular bus services link Ambleside with the railway station at Windermere. Less frequent bus services link Glenridding with the railway station at Penrith

Red Screes seen from Wansfell

DAY ONE

Leave Ambleside by heading up the Kirkstone Road, known locally as 'The Struggle', because of its steep gradient. In the nineteenth century travellers had to step down from their horse-drawn carriages and walk up the first section. Pass the turnings to Low and High Sweden Bridges and a turning on the right to Roundhill Farm. Shortly a path leads north-west across the hillside, just to the south-east of a small wood. A broad and grassy ridge continues to Red Screes with the views over Ambleside growing larger and more extensive all the time.

The summit cairn and trig point on Red Screes is perched near the edge of a steep escarpment sweeping down to the Kirkstone Pass, so not surprisingly the views are some of the finest in South Lakeland. A steep and rather tricky descent leads you to the Kirkstone Pass Inn, which is the highest in the Lake District at 454m (1489ft) above sea-level.

Stony Cove Pike beckons, so take the path over St Raven's Edge and Caudale Moor to its summit. A steep descent and re-ascent across Threshthwaite Mouth takes you to the columnar cairn of Thornthwaite Crag, where you may catch sight of the wild ponies that roam these fells. The high point of the walk is now reached by swinging north-east on a clear path to High Street at 828m (2716ft). The main path bypasses the summit, so leave it for the tumbledown stone wall along the crest of the fell and you'll find a trig point marking the summit.

A Roman road, linking forts at Brougham near Penrith with forts around Windermere and Ambleside, at one time traversed the crest of High Street and was the highest such road in England. At later dates in its history, horse races were held up here,

ALONG THE WAY

The **Hinkler Memorial** on the summit of Helvellyn commemorates the successful first landing and take-off by aeroplane on Helvellyn in 1926 by John Leeming and Bert Hinkler. The ascent of **Helvellyn** via **Striding Edge** is one of the Lake District's classic routes. The ridge is narrow, with lofty views over Nethermost Cove and Red Tarn. The ridge can be followed either along its crest or more easily on a slightly lower path on the Red Tarn side.

Caudale Moor's southern slopes are known as John Bell's Banner. The name originates from Rev John Bell, a schoolmaster of Ambleside, who lived from 1553 to 1620. Banner is the old name for a boundary and since the parishes of Windermere, Grasmere and Patterdale met on

Caudale Moor, it is probable that the nearest summit became known as John Bell's Banner after the area's reverend.

Until the early nineteenth century, the smooth grassy top of **High Street** was the venue of the annual Mardale shepherds' meet, during which shepherds would identify and retrieve stray sheep. Later the event became a festive occasion with sporting events such as horse racing, wrestling and fell running.

so that High Street is also known as Racecourse Hill.

A steady descent north to The Knott takes you on a clear path past Angle Tarn and its neighbouring Pikes to finally emerge at Boredale Hause, where a clear path descends to Patterdale.

DAY TWO

The return leg begins with an ascent of Striding Edge, an airy ridge walk with steep drops on both sides, so it's not for the faint-hearted! A number of paths climb to Grisedale Brow, from where you begin the crossing of Striding Edge. Here walkers often congregate to take a bite to eat before making the famous traverse. Those who are new to 'the ridge' sit quiet and pensive, while the 'old hands' recall previous trips in foul weather or fine.

Navigation is never a problem on Striding Edge, you simply stick to the crest, or perhaps follow a lower path to the north, which is wise in winter or high winds. Both routes meet at a narrow rocky cleft and here there is no easy way, you just have to climb down it, facing in or facing out or bouncing on your bum.

The summit shelter of Helvellyn is reached after a scrubby scramble from the end of Striding Edge. Throughout this section there are memorials and stories to investigate, all adding to the Helvellyn saga. The way home is south from Helvellyn, over the broad plateau of Nethermost Pike and around the rocky turret of Dollywagon Pike. A steep zigzagging descent then deposits you shaken and stirred at Grisedale Tarn.

A stiff pull on to Deepdale Hause gives access to Fairfield via Stony Cove Pike. But don't dash off; a short walk to St Sunday Crag's summit is worthy of your effort, for this is the connoisseurs' mountain, where the finest views abound.

Retrace your steps to Deepdale Hause and continue over Cofa Pike to the summit of Fairfield. Take a final look back to Helvellyn and then begin the walk down half of the Fairfield Horseshoe to Ambleside. It matters not which arm of the Horseshoe that you tackle. I favour the route over Hart Crag, High Pike and Low Pike, as this has less road walking back to Ambleside at the end, but there are equally good reasons to descend via Great Rigg and Heron Pike.

PATTERDALE TO SHAP

Mardale Ill Bell from High Street with Harter Fell beyond

This is a walk that takes in most of the major summits of the eastern fells as well as parts of the famous Coast-to-Coast walk, with walkers making a traverse from the heart of the Lake District in Patterdale to the fringe at Shap. Between these boundaries rise the wild, remote and rolling eastern fells. In places these fells are popular but in other areas you can enjoy the solitude far from other walkers, civilisation and clear footpaths. Along the way there are extensive views and steps into history as you cross the route of one of the most famous Roman roads in the Lake District on High Street and follow the shore of Haweswater Reservoir, whose waters have been made artificially high by the building of a dam at the northern end of the valley. Finally there are the remote eastern moors and Sleddale valley where Lakeland shepherds used to drive their sheep and cattle to market on a regular basis.

DAY ONE

A path climbs from Patterdale to Boredale Hause and this brings your first views back across the Ullswater valley to Fairfield and the Helvellyn range, which form a formidable barrier to the west. You are on part of Wainwright's Coast-to-Coast path and the passage of feet have made navigation easy, so simply follow the track south towards Angletarn Pikes. This is a wonderful walk as the path is narrow and clings to the steep fellside, revealing views ahead towards the Fairfield range of hills once again and down to Brotherswater in the valley.

Wind your way around Angletarn Pikes, which

aren't climbed on this walk. Angle Tarn itself is a popular place for picnickers who want a taste of wilderness, but there is better to come so don't linger too long beside the lapping waters. A steady climb continues to Satura Crags, where views down Bannerdale are worth stopping for before you tackle a final short climb to The Knott. You have now reached the ridge of the High Street massif, although you don't visit the high point of the ridge today as it is a fair walk in the wrong direction and ties in more naturally with the return journey on day two.

WALK FACTS

Start/Finish	Patterdale, GR 396158
Distance	Day one: 24km (15 miles)
	Day two: 26km (16 miles)
Total ascent	Day one: 770m (2526ft)
	Day two: 1000m (3280ft)
Time	Day one: 9 hours
	Day two: 10 hours

Difficulty A long, high-level walk with mainly clear paths but some difficult navigation on some of the less well used areas and a lot of hill climbing throughout

Accommodation Campsites and B&Bs in Patterdale, Glenridding and Shap. Youth hostels in Patterdale and Glenridding

Public transport Limited bus services to Shap from Penrith, with very limited connections to Kendal. Regular bus service to Glenridding and Patterdale with connections to the railway station at Penrith

ALONG THE WAY

The bridleway through **Sleddale** formed part of a system of drove roads that existed throughout the Lake District. These were used to move cattle and sheep as early as the Middle Ages and reached a peak in the early nineteenth century. Around 200 cattle or 2,000 sheep would be moved at a time, covering only around six or twelve miles in a day. But overall the distances covered were great and it was not uncommon for Galloway cattle to be driven all the way to London before being sold at a market.

The drove road through Sleddale was a local route that was used to move herds to the main drove roads of Britain that extended north to south from Scotland to London, passing Shap and the fringe of Cumbria along the way. When the railways arrived at Shap in 1855, droving virtually stopped as cattle and sheep were then moved by rail.

Mardale was a beautiful and secluded valley, but it was partially lost when the valley was flooded in the winter of 1936–37 to provide a water supply for the city of Manchester. There used to be a village in the valley, also called Mardale, and this lacked a church of its own until 1729, so the dead had to be carried to Shap on horseback by way of a corpse road that climbed over Mardale Common and Swindale. There are many such corpse roads throughout the Lake District and many provide useful walking routes to this day.

The Coast-to-Coast path descends east over Kidsty Pike to the shore of Haweswater, but our route heads north-east for High Raise along the main ridge which formed part of the course taken by a Roman road that linked their forts near Penrith with those near Ambleside. The going is easy to Loadpot Hill. Its isolated position provides views in all directions and as it lies just off the beaten track, few walkers venture here.

But there is much of interest including the remains of Lowther House chimney, a former shooting lodge.

Pick up a faint path east to Low Kop and descend to the banks of Measand Beck and The Forces waterfall. A broad track carries you along the shore of Haweswater Reservoir to Burnbanks. It's now a case of linking footpaths to reach Naddle Bridge and the banks of Haweswater Beck to High Bark Barn. Here

the path crosses fields to Rawhead Farm and Rosgill Bridge. Signs lead to Shap Abbey only a short walk from Shap itself where there is plenty of accommodation available.

DAY TWO

The return journey is quite remote and in places pathless, so good navigation skills are essential. Leave Shap via Keld and then keep an eye on the map as you head south-west from Keld, around Brown Hill, across an access road to Stack House. Things improve from Stack House as the path, now a bridleway, becomes clearer and leads along the southern flank of Great Ladstones. A steady climb, with Sleddale valley way down to the left, ultimately leads to the wilds of a rough plateau above Mosedale. Again the going becomes tough as the path loses its identity and you have to find a way down to Mosedale Beck which is crossed by a bridge. Things improve once more, as the bridleway leading west through Mosedale is fairly clear for a while. But all too soon the going gets difficult again as you climb out of Mosedale and down

Brotherswater from Angletarn Pikes

to Brownhowe Bottom at the head of Longsleddale. At last there's a clear path and this takes you north to Gatesgarth Pass from where a stiff climb scales Harter Fell. This is the first summit of the day, but you will have used plenty of navigating skill getting here, so linger a while and take in the view to High Street and Haweswater.

There's a very steep descent to Nan Bield Pass, where a stone wind-break provides a welcome shelter before the long haul over Mardale Ill Bell takes you to the highest point of the walk on High Street. This is also the highest point in the Eastern Fells and the view is of an equally high standard.

To end the day, leave High Street by walking south-west around the head of Hayeswater to Thornthwaite Crag, which is clearly identified from afar by its large summit cairn built on a rocky plinth. A steep and rough descent leads down to Threshthwaite Mouth to Hartsop and the end of the walk at Patterdale is now well within your stride.

STAVELEY TO SHAP

The fringe of the Lake District is often disregarded by walkers who instead head for the heart of the National Park. But there is good walking in these outlying areas, particularly for those who enjoy unfrequented paths and wild moors. The boundary line of the Lake District almost links Staveley with Shap and it is the area between these two points that this walk explores. There are a number of high fells within this area but most have few if any paths and you'll find yourself heather-bashing if you attempt to bag their summits. Therefore this walk follows a series of low-level paths and bridleways, many of which were once used as trade routes, drovers roads and old coach roads. A few minor peaks are climbed along the way where good paths exist and these provide extensive views over the rolling fells of this remote corner.

WALK FACTS

Start/Finish Staveley, GR 470982
Distance Day one: 27km (17 miles)
Day two: 22.5km (14 miles)
Total ascent Day one: 600m (1968ft)
Day two: 600m (1968ft)
Time Day one: 9 hours
Day two: 8 hours
Difficulty A long but straightforward walk on clear paths mainly at low level through valleys with very little ascent
Accommodation B&Bs, hotels and campsite at Staveley and Shap
Public transport Regular bus services link Staveley with Windermere and Kendal and there are railway stations at these places. Less frequent bus services link Shap with Kendal and Penrith, where there's also a railway station

Bridge over the River Sprint in Longsleddale

DAY ONE

You'll need good map reading skills throughout this walk to link all the footpaths and lanes and the work begins straightaway in Staveley, where you need to walk north out of the village, following signs for Kentmere. You can cross the River Kent at Barley Bridge to follow a track through fields around Piked Howe to Littlewood Farm. Birk Field and Potter Tarn are close by and these bring fine views across the fringe of the Lake District towards Kendal, an area where stone walls bisect every green expanse of land into a patchwork of fields, where sheep and cattle huddle together under a solitary tree or beside a wall to find shelter from the elements. These views stay with you as you descend from Potter Fell. Take care here to find a path that leaves the lane at a sharp right-hand bend, your route continuing straight ahead for Garnett Bridge.

The first real hill of the day is Whiteside Pike and the climb to its summit begins from the farm at Murthwaite in Longsleddale. A track from here takes

Opposite: Longsleddale from Buckbarrow Crag

ALONG THE WAY

Staveley was a busy industrial village and the centre of Lakeland's bobbin industry from the end of the eighteenth century to the beginning of the nineteenth. The village stood astride the main road into Lakeland in those days. Now the bobbin industry has gone and a bypass keeps traffic out of the narrow streets. Today most people who pass through Staveley are bound for Kentmere and the high fells. Few give it a second glance.

Shap was at one time home to a flourishing market town, a busy railway station and a world-famous supply of granite. Cattle and sheep were driven here along the drovers' routes from all over Cumbria, while herds of animals from Scotland also passed through Shap on their way to the markets in Lancashire and as far south as London.

   Today only the granite remains and the town takes much of its income from Coast-to-Coast walkers who are following Wainwright's famous 200-mile walk between St Bees Head on the west coast of Cumbria and Robin Hood's Bay on the east coast of Yorkshire. There are campsites and B&Bs in profusion but take care not to arrive on Thursdays or Fridays as this is when most of the Coast-to-Coast walkers reach Shap, and you may find all the accommodation full during high season.

you across open fields dotted with sheep to a lane, where you turn left for the climb to Whiteside Pike. The rocky summit of the fell brings wonderful views and includes most of the eastern fells. You may be tempted to follow the ridge north-west around the head of Bannisdale and although this is perfectly possible, it's very hard work as there are few paths and

a lot of sheep tracks to follow through the heather.
   You leave the summit of Whiteside Pike by descending east across the open fell and rough pasture to Dryhowe Bridge. A track continues to Thorn Cottage, from where an old coach road takes you alongside the A6 main road and this can be followed almost all the way to Shap. The most dangerous part

of the day comes when you need to cross the main road in an attempt to follow the original line of the old coach road as it heads past Hollowgate to High Borrow Bridge. But the walking is generally easy now, although sometimes there are boggy sections where the old road has fallen into disrepair. As you walk keep a look-out for milestones, a ruined staging post building and the Wasdale Old Bridge, a seventeenth century packhorse bridge.

The old coach road leads along the fringe of the Lake District to the end of some woods where you can turn left to Shap Lodge. Again you must take your life in your hands as you cross the A6. The final section to Shap links lanes and paths across the rough pasture of Low Fell to Wet Sleddale Reservoir. A lane then takes you over Wickers Gill towards Kemp Howe, from where footpaths can be traced to Shap via Steps Hall.

DAY TWO

You now leave the boundary of the Lake District for the heart of the eastern fells. On the whole the return leg is very easy, although as usual getting out of the town will take longer than anticipated. To make it easier follow signs to Shap Abbey and then pick up paths to Keld. Your eventual destination is Swindale but you'll need to follow a series of paths through Keld and Tailbert before you can join a path around Langhowe Pike and across Swindale Beck. Navigation eases here as you simply follow a lane above the beck to Swindale Head. There's then a bridleway that leads out of the head of the valley onto the soggy plateau of Mosedale.

A clear path is joined in Longsleddale. This is a popular path for walkers heading for the high fells, but at one time it was a major drovers' route through the Lake District. The track is broad and hemmed in on both sides by stone walls and you can well imagine huge herds of sheep or cattle being driven through the valley.

The walled lane leads to Sadgill, a popular spot for tourists and picnickers, so expect a few cars to be parked near the bridge. The bridleway continues over the River Sprint and out of the valley to Cocklaw Fell. Behind there are fine views back down the valley and across the eastern fells. The path leads past Skeggles Water and then begins its descent to Staveley via Brunt Fell and Park House. To avoid a road walk, follow footpaths to High House, Ghyll Bank, Littlewood Farm and Barley Bridge which leaves just a short road walk into Staveley remaining.

HAWESWATER SKYLINE

The Haweswater Reservoir is a man-made feature that lies in the palm of a ring of fells, which all provide fine viewpoints from which to take in this expanse of water, which hides the village of Mardale Green beneath its waves. This walk makes a high-level traverse of these fells to give a unique opportunity for the walker to study Haweswater from every angle. The valley of Mardale and its principal village Mardale Green were lost when the dam was built to the west of Burnbanks over fifty years ago. Today all that remains is a road running the length of the reservoir which terminates at a car park at Mardale Head. Mardale is a quiet backwater of Lakeland, even though the number of cars at Mardale Head may initially make you think otherwise. But get away from the valley and you can easily find solitude on these fells.

DAY ONE

If you plan ahead you can save your shoulders by dropping off your spare clothes and wash bag at your accommodation in Bampton Grange, during the drive through to the start of this walk. So there's no reason for carrying a heavy sack unless you really like making things tough for yourself!

From the car park at Mardale Head a footpath climbs south-west up towards Small Water, a wonderful patch of water nestling under the high fells. The path winds around the shore and up to Nan Bield Pass, where a stone shelter provides a welcome wind-break from the elements which soar up Kentmere. The views back over Haweswater are good from here but there are better to come so don't linger too long.

WALK FACTS

Start/Finish	Mardale Head, GR 46910
Distance	Day one: 16km (10 miles)
	Day two: 17.7km (11 miles)
Total ascent	Day one: 750m (2460ft)
	Day two: 750m (2460ft)
Time	Day one: 6 hours
	Day two: 6½ hours

Difficulty A moderate walk with many clear paths to follow as well as some walking over rough unpathed terrain, so some map reading skills are required particularly on day one

Accommodation B&Bs and hotels in Bampton Grange and down the Mardale valley

Public transport Very limited bus services extend to the start of this walk from Penrith in summer. A limited bus service also extends to Burnbanks, again from the nearest railway station at Penrith

Head south-east from Nan Bield Pass up the steep slopes of Harter Fell. The views grow on every step and you'll soon be thinking that Haweswater Reservoir is beautiful even though it is man-made. The views also include the whole High Street range of fells that you'll traverse on day two. The views of Haweswater slip away as you cross the plateau of Harter Fell and your attention is grabbed by the strange summit cairn which includes remains of a boundary fence protruding from the rocks.

A fence line leads to Gatesgarth Pass, where footpaths cross this path from the north, south, east and west. Your route is up, along the side of a fence to Branstree, but you'll see the best views from Artle Crag Pike just to one side of the main summit.

Now a fence line provides a welcome aid to navigation as you walk to Selside Pike and across the Old Corpse Road linking Swindale to Mardale. This track was originally used to take the dead on horseback to Shap for burial, but it hasn't been used for such purposes since 1736. Today it is more often lively walkers who use the route. Unpathed terrain continues to Powley's Hill and Harper Hill, from where you can join a bridleway leading north-east down to Naddle Farm and the main road through Mardale. A short road walk takes you to your overnight accommodation at Bampton Grange.

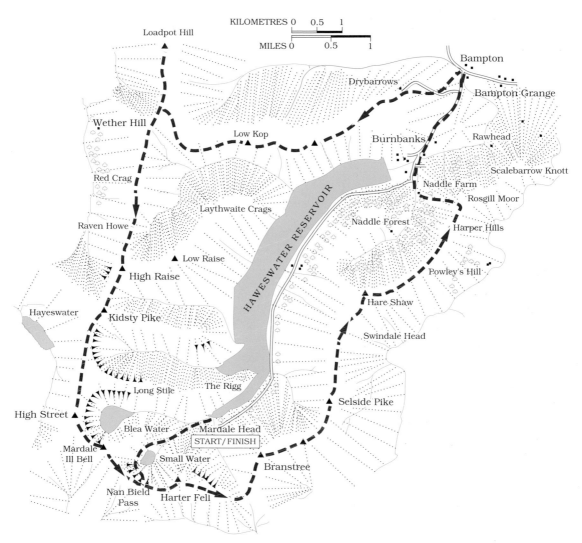

KILOMETRES 0   0.5   1
MILES 0   0.5   1

Loadpot Hill

Drybarrows

Bampton

Bampton Grange

Wether Hill

Low Kop

Burnbanks

Rawhead

Red Crag

Scalebarrow Knott

HAWESWATER RESERVOIR

Naddle Farm

Rosgill Moor

Laythwaite Crags

Naddle Forest

Harper Hills

Raven Howe

Low Raise

Powley's Hill

High Raise

Hare Shaw

Hayeswater

Kidsty Pike

Swindale Head

Long Stile

The Rigg

Selside Pike

High Street

Blea Water

Mardale Head

START/FINISH

Mardale Ill Bell

Small Water

Branstree

Nan Bield Pass

Harter Fell

ALONG THE WAY

Bampton was famous for its eighteenth century grammar school. It was not so much that there was a grammar school in such a small village but that it stood out as a fine school even when compared to such schools as Appleby. Today Bampton is famous for the Mardale Shepherd's Meet, which is held at the end of autumn. The meeting is used to return sheep to their rightful owners after they have become separated from their flocks on the fells during the year. Every area of the Lake District has such meetings, but the Mardale meeting is the most famous. The Meet was originally held at Mardale village, but this was lost under the Haweswater Reservoir which was created in the 1930s by damming Haweswater Beck to expand the former lake into a flooded valley. According to literature and photographs of the time, Mardale was a long, green valley rather like Longsleddale. In dry summers, such as in 1976, the ruins of the old village can sometimes be seen and you can even walk between fields and over a stone bridge that spanned Haweswater Beck.

HAWESWATER SKYLINE

*Below: Blea Water from High Street with Haweswater
Reservoir in the distance*

DAY TWO

To save your back, you can leave your heavy rucksack
in your B&B and pick it up on the way back through
Bampton Grange at the end of the walk. The return
leg takes you down the north-western side of
Haweswater. But the first problem is getting to the
high fells from Bampton Grange. The OS Outdoor
Leisure (1:25,000) map is ideal for this section and
makes route finding easy from Bampton Grange to
Bampton and then across Bampton Bridge over
Howes Beck to Drybarrows.

You are now on a fell path which carries you
steadily up to Low Kop and Wether Hill. To get some
fine views, head north to Loadpot Hill if you can bear
the thought of going slightly off route for a while. You
are now on the High Street range of fells and Loadpot
Hill is the last major summit to the north, which allows
it extensive views. These are a great improvement over
those from neighbouring Wether Hill. The walk south
follows the course of the famous Roman road that once
existed here and was built to link forts near Penrith

with those near Ambleside. The main path bypasses
Kidsty Pike, but a short diversion to this summit
provides unique views across Riggindale to the eastern
escarpment of High Street. This is also a fine place to
take lunch as you drink in the view.

To reach High Street you can either follow the
tumbledown stone wall or trace the cliff edge. The
latter option is more spectacular and ensures that you
witness the finest views, which may even include a
golden eagle riding the thermals above Riggindale.
High Street, the highest point in the eastern fells of
the Lake District, is rather disappointing at first. The
reason is that High Street's summit is very broad and
its summit cairn is not well placed to get the best
views. To make the most of the fell, wander around a
bit and head for the edges so that you can see beyond
the plateau beneath your feet.

To end the walk, stay on the main path around to
Mardale Ill Bell to Nan Bield Pass, where you can
descend past Small Water to the car park at Mardale
Head.

ULLSWATER SKYLINE

The Ullswater valley is home to Lakeland's finest lake, Ullswater, which is squeezed between the Helvellyn range to the west and the High Street range of fells to the east. The foothills of Ullswater fill the gap between the great lake and the mountains and although these fells are not as shapely nor as grand as either of their neighbours, they provide fine views and wonderful walking. There are also waterfalls to visit and wild open moors to cross. This walk takes in many of the finest features in the Ullswater valley during its mid-level circumnavigation of the lake.

Ferry on Ullswater

DAY ONE

You can ease the burden of your rucksack by dropping your heaviest gear off at Glenridding before setting off from Pooley Bridge. The walk begins with a road walk from Pooley Bridge to Roehead, so take the Howtown Road past the church. If you cross the main road at a junction and continue in the same direction you'll be climbing onto the fell, where you'll come across a cairn that marks the point where the High Street Roman road descends from Loadpot Hill. Here you turn right to follow the Roman road, as it heads south-west over the High Street range.

If you are well versed in navigation you could leave the main path for Arthur's Pike and descend a little over its western flank to get views into the Ullswater valley. But as there is no clear path linking the Roman road with the summit of Arthur's Pike, you may prefer to stick with the main route to Loadpot Hill. There are great views from here over the plains of north Cumbria, as this is the final major summit in the High Street range. Just south from the summit there are the remains of Louther House, a former shooting lodge.

You need to leave Loadpot Hill in a northerly direction for Bonscale Pike, where a series of three stone pillars stand, the lower of which is Bonscale Tower, with a tremendous view over Ullswater. A grassy groove descends down the fellside towards Howtown, a small village served by boat from Pooley Bridge and Glenridding, which makes it a popular destination for an afternoon's walk. The road through Howtown climbs up a series of zigzags towards Martindale. St Peter's Church stands at the top of the road and to the right there's Hallin Fell, which offers extensive views down Ullswater to the northern fringe of the Lake District, making its ascent well worth the diversion.

From St Peter's Church continue down the road towards Martindale, and take a path on the right that

WALK FACTS

Start/Finish Pooley Bridge, GR 471245
Distance   Day one: 23km (14.5 miles)
                Day two: 21km (13 miles)
Total ascent Day one: 1170m (3838ft)
                Day two: 1020m (3347ft)
Time   Day one: 8 hours
                Day two: 8 hours
Difficulty A straightforward mid-level fell walk with generally clear paths to follow but also some short sections of unpathed fell where good map reading skills will be needed
Accommodation B&Bs, campsites and hotels at Pooley Bridge, Patterdale and Glenridding, with youth hostels at Patterdale and Glenridding
Public transport Regular bus services link the Ullswater valley with the railway station at Penrith. A ferry links Glenridding with Howtown and Pooley Bridge

Previous page: Ullswater from St Sunday Crag
Opposite: Ullswater from Howtown

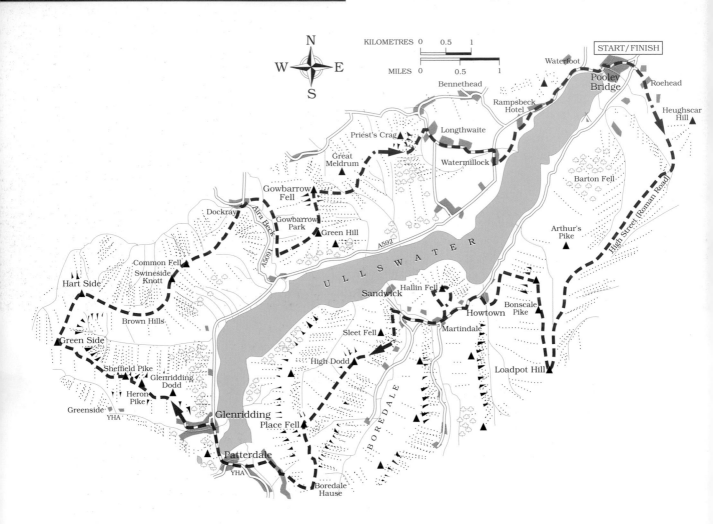

ALONG THE WAY

Pooley Bridge is set in flat, open countryside at the foot of Ullswater – ideal for gentle countryside strolling. The village consists of grey stone houses, a couple of hotels and a few tourist shops. The name 'Pooley' is Norse for 'the hill with a pool'. The hill that the name refers to is the conical Dunmallet Hill that lies just beside the village and this was also the site of an iron age fort. The 'Bridge' part of the name was added in 1800.

Aira Force, five miles north of Glenridding on the western shores of Ullswater, is probably the Lake District's most famous waterfall. The spectacular series of cascades are collectively known by the name of the largest, which drops 21m (70ft) down a wooded ravine. Bridges cross the waterfalls to provide spectacular views. To the east of Aira Force rises Gowbarrow Park where a drift of daffodils provided inspiration to William Wordsworth on 15 April 1802. The famous poet was walking with his sister, Dorothy, and on their return William wrote his famous poem which began:

I wandered lonely as a cloud
That floats on high o'er vales and hills,
When all at once I saw a crowd,
A host, of golden daffodils;
Beside the lake, beneath the trees,
Fluttering and dancing in the breeze.

leads above Hause Farm to Hallin Bank and finally Bridge End. A bridge takes you over Sandwick Beck and then you need to pick your way through paths and lanes to climb over the lower slopes of Sleet Fell towards Boredale before reaching High Dodd and then the summit of Place Fell. This is a fine viewpoint once again, particularly to the north and the head of Ullswater. The Ullswater valley is now very close, with a short walk down to Boredale Hause leading to Patterdale and Glenridding.

DAY TWO

The route followed from Glenridding back to Pooley Bridge is very interesting and takes in a number of lower fells with views to the higher fells and Ullswater. Your first objective is to escape from Glenridding onto Glenridding Dodd, a rather underestimated summit. You need to leave Glenridding by following signs, 'Bridleway Greenside Mine Keppel Cove'. At a cattle grid near some cottages, a path climbs uphill beside a dry beck to Glenridding Dodd, with its cairn and fine views of Ullswater and the eastern fells. Follow cairns up to Heron Pike, where there is a metal post with the markings M1912 and H1912 on its sides, which marked the boundary between the Marshal estate of Patterdale and the Howard estate of Greystokes.

A peaty depression carries you to Sheffield Pike, with its particularly impressive views to the Helvellyn massif and the Greenside mines, one of England's most productive lead mines in the past. Heading west and then north from Sheffield Pike you cross the broad, grassy ridge to Hart Side. A faint track leads all the way to the summit which has three cairns and views to Great Mell Fell, a conical summit to the north. From Hart Side walk south-east over unpathed grassy fells towards Glencoyne and join the Brown Hills ridge to Swineside Knott, where there are more great views to Ullswater. Stay on the rough ridge to reach Common Fell, from where Dockray is reached by a rough track.

At Dockray you join the A5091 and turn left to cross Aira Beck. A path continues to Aira Force waterfall, a magnificent 21m (70ft) high multiple fall with viewing bridges over the brink. After studying the falls return to the higher stone-arched bridge and turn left to climb up the craggy knoll of Gowbarrow Fell, with yet more fine views over Ullswater to the mighty eastern fells of High Street. A path leads east past the remains of a shooting lodge and then below Great Meldrum and Little Meldrum to eventually arrive at the road below Priest's Crag. Turn right here then follow paths and lanes to Watermillock, Rampsbeck Hotel and Pooley Bridge via the A592 road.

THRELKELD TO GLENRIDDING

Helvellyn is the highest point on a spine of mountains that extends through the heart of the Lake District, north to south. The two sides of the range are distinctly different, particularly around the area of Helvellyn's summit. To the west, the slopes are smooth with few crags, gullies, gills or escarpments. These slopes provide fairly easy ascents to the tops and indeed the most popular route onto Helvellyn begins from the western slopes. Conversely the eastern slopes of the Helvellyn range are riven with cliffs, gullies and rocky ridges, where the flow of ice has bitten into the mountain to leave interesting and intricate routes for the adventurous walker. This route visits both sides of the Helvellyn range starting from Threlkeld, its northern tip, and travelling to Glenridding under the steep eastern cliffs of Helvellyn.

DAY ONE

Threlkeld is largely bypassed by tourists but with a stunning view onto Clough Head, the northern outpost of the Helvellyn range, and with Blencathra on the village doorstep, Threlkeld must be a fine place to live and indeed a fine place to start a walk.

You can see your target, Clough Head, from the roadside. To get there you have to walk south down the B5322 into St John's in the Vale, a delightful valley of lush pastoral scenery that seems almost like another world, with only a narrow winding lane and a river twisting between fields of stone walls, sheep and cattle. A zigzagging path carries you up onto Clough Head and its summit cairn. There are excellent views from here to Blencathra, while the Helvellyn range stretches south as far as the eye can see. The hard

WALK FACTS

Start/Finish	Threlkeld, GR 320253
Distance	Day one: 15km (9.3 miles)
	Day two: 20km (12.4 miles)
Total ascent	Day one: 900m (2953ft)
	Day two: 1100m (3609ft)
Time	Day one: 6 hours
	Day two: 8 hours

Difficulty A high-level fell walk, with a narrow airy walk over Striding Edge, but this can be avoided by easier paths. Clear paths throughout
Accommodation Youth hostels, B&B and campsites down St John's Vale, Glenridding, only B&Bs at Threlkeld
Public transport There are regular bus services between Keswick and Threlkeld and the railway station at Penrith. Regular bus services also extend to Glenridding from Penrith

work is now over, so turn your back on Blencathra and walk along the rolling grass to the strange rocky island of Calfhow Pike before heading east to Great Dodd. Watson's Dodd comes next and then Stybarrow Dodd, which marks the last of the Dodd range of summits. It's been fairly easy walking so far and there is little change as you start your descent east from Sticks Pass. This is the highest pass in the Lake District in regular use at 738m (2420ft). In Elizabethan times, it was used regularly for the carriage of lead by pack ponies to Keswick. The path leads through the Greenside mines to Glenridding, where a wide variety of accommodation awaits your arrival.

DAY TWO

The return journey to Threlkeld via Striding Edge and Helvellyn is more strenuous and longer than day one. To begin you need to gain the slopes of Striding Edge, the long, narrow, rocky arm that extends east from Helvellyn's summit to the doorstep of Glenridding. So take the path from Glenridding Bridge at the centre of the village down the south side of Glenridding Beck to Westside. From here a path continues around Lanty's Tarn to Grisedale. The path descends and then starts to climb a little as it traverses the Grisedale valley. A westerly climb takes you onto the crest of Striding Edge, which is

ALONG THE WAY

St John's Vale has been the site of a number of major floods and in 1749 many of the bridges, houses and a corn mill were swept away. To prevent further problems many of the buildings were placed well above the low level and flat valley floor and the river itself has built up banks which should ease future problems.

St John's Church, from which the valley takes its name, stands isolated on the high ground between High Rigg and Low Rigg so that it may also serve the neighbouring Naddle Valley. John Richardson (1817–1886) a famous Cumberland dialect poet, is buried here. His unusual spelling of words in his poems paints a clear picture of the dales folk who lived in the area during the nineteenth century.

Castle Rock of Triermain rises at the southern end of St John's Vale and is clearly visible from High Rigg. There are some ruins on the rock from Eadulf's Castle which existed here in the thirteenth century, but it appears that this was only a look-out pele-tower rather than a fortified castle.

The rock was visited by Sir Walter Scott in 1797 and inspired his poem of 1805 *The Bridal of Triermain*: a tale of how King Arthur comes to the castle, finds it deserted and blows the bugle hanging outside. The castle then comes alive with flashing lights and a 'band of damsels fair' who hold King Arthur enthralled until he is able to finally tear himself away. It is this poem that gave the rock its name 'of Triermain' as it was formerly known simply as Castle Rock.

Below: Helvellyn in snow above Thirlmere valley seen from High Rigg

met at Hole-in-the-Wall, a popular place to stop and have a quick brew before tackling the ridge.

There are two principal routes along Striding Edge. The purists way is to follow the crest, stepping gingerly from airy block to airy block. But in high winds, snow, heavy rain or when you are just plain terrified, it's safer to follow a lower path that makes a traverse of the northern face above Red Tarn. Both routes meet at the delightfully named Bad Step – a steep but short rocky gully to climb down. It only takes a couple of moves but it can be tricky for the inexperienced and queues are known on busy weekends.

If you can get yourself down the Bad Step, your reward is a steep haul up onto the summit of Helvellyn. But that's the hard work over and there's a huge wind-break where you can find shelter from the wind and possibly rain. Helvellyn brings wonderful views, as you'd expect from the Lake District's third highest mountain at 950m (3117ft) above sea-level.

Leave Helvellyn by walking north-west to Lower Man and then descend the short narrow ridge towards

A lone walker on Striding Edge, with Helvellyn summit to the right

Whiteside Bank, taking care not to descend down Swirral Edge by mistake, which heads north-east from near the Helvellyn summit. You now leave those steep cliffs and narrow ridges behind for the ease of walking over rolling grass to Raise, a rarely visited outlying summit.

Shortly you'll arrive at Sticks Pass (for the second time on the walk), but this time you turn left to descend into the mouth of St John's in the Vale. For a final flurry of hill walking, walk along the A591 towards Keswick, cross St John's Beck and then follow a path over a stile onto High Rigg. This offers splendid views of Castle Rock of Triermain and over Thirlmere to Raven Crag with Helvellyn towering overhead. The ridge leads north through pine and oak woods and down to the Diocesan Youth Centre and church. If you cross the road here and continue up and over Low Rigg you can easily follow a series of footpaths back to Threlkeld.

Below: View north from Scout Scar, near Kendal; Langdale Pikes in the distance

KENDAL TO NEWBY BRIDGE

The Lyth and Winster valleys dominate the heart of the region between Lake Windermere and Kendal. Although there are no dramatic crags or particularly picturesque villages, this is where you can walk quietly along wooded lanes and paths, among spring blossom and hedgerows, while passing through tiny villages and over rolling countryside of fields and wooded groves.

The great limestone block of Whitbarrow separates the Lyth valley from the Winster valley. This 200m (656ft) high escarpment is topped by a fine limestone pavement and the view from the top is well worth the climb. To the east of the Lyth valley rises Scout Scar, another fine limestone escarpment which provides an extensive view over the whole area covered by this walk between Kendal and Newby Bridge.

WALK FACTS

Start/Finish	Kendal, GR 515925
Distance	Day one: 25km (15.6 miles)
	Day two: 17km (10.6 miles)
Total ascent	Day one: 600m (1968ft)
	Day two: 400m (1312ft)
Time	Day one: 9 hours
	Day two: 6 hours

Difficulty Straightforward low-level walking along country lanes, field paths and forests, some careful navigation required to trace all the inter-linked paths

Accommodation Hotels, B&Bs and youth hostels at Kendal, limited B&Bs at Newby Bridge

Public transport Regular bus and rail services to Kendal. Regular bus services to Newby Bridge from the railway stations at Ulverston and Grange over Sands

DAY ONE

Kendal is well served by public transport and its railway station has regular connections to the west coast main line, making it an ideal starting point for this walk. The town stands just outside the National Park boundary but it is still the administrative centre for south Lakeland. To escape the town, head for Abbott Hall car park in the main street and follow the

ALONG THE WAY

Winster valley's western side is formed by Newton and Cartmel Fells and is composed of Silurian slate, while the limestone block of Whitbarrow provides the eastern boundary of the valley. The contrast between the two is striking, as the land form changes from smooth, rolling slopes of dark slate to steep escarpments of white limestone.

Whitbarrow has a nature reserve on top known as Flodder Allotment. The term allotment is used as valley farms share out the fellside between them and there are a number in the area.

Kendal is famous for its Mint Cake, but it was once a centre of the woollen industry. The town was also famous for the Kendal Bowmen, skilled archers clad in Kendal Green cloth who fought the Scots at the battle of Flodden Field in 1513. Catherine Parr, the last of Henry VIII's wives lived at Kendal Castle in the sixteenth century before she became Queen of England. Kendal is also distinctive for its series of named and numbered yards that are tucked away down alleyways and through arches and these were once the focus of the local fishing industry.

The small village of **Winster** has a scattering of whitewashed stone cottages and the River Winster, which flows through the centre of the village, formed the border between the old counties of Westmorland and Lancashire, before the counties were rearranged in 1974.

road opposite which leads west out of town. Following signs for Underbarrow you will reach the edge of Scout Scar, but leave it for the moment as you visit this superb feature on your return. Instead take a track on the right that leads to Cunswick Scar, which is really the northern extent of Scout Scar. With fine views to the north and west over the rolling fields of the upper Lyth valley, your route traces footpaths and lanes across the B5284 to Moss Side, Rather Heath and Ashes.

You join the Dales Way for a short distance and may meet walkers who have travelled the whole route of the 130km (81 miles) long-distance path that starts in Ilkley in Yorkshire and ends in Bowness in Cumbria. With clear waymarking, the going is easy as you make your way past Waingap, where you leave the Dales Way for footpaths through Boxtree and Sunnybrow. A complex series of paths and lanes takes you over the B5284 to Winster and the crossing of the A5074. You have to follow country lanes between the fields through Winster House and south to the end of Moor How, where footpaths can be joined once again as you climb up for fine views over Windermere to the west and the Winster valley to the east. Sadly there is no right-of-way along the ridge to Gummer's How, so you must follow a path east from the woods to the minor road that links Crosthwaite to Newby Bridge. If you follow this road towards Newby Bridge for about one mile you can take a path on the right that climbs to the summit of Gummer's How and it's well worth the effort, for the view over Windermere is outstanding.

To end the day simply retrace your steps to the road and follow it downhill into Newby Bridge.

DAY TWO

The return journey to Kendal crosses the flat-bottomed Winster and Lyth valleys and also climbs the great limestone escarpments of Whitbarrow Scar and Scout Scar, making it a tremendous walk. The day begins with a walk to Staveley-in-Cartmel, not to be confused with the larger Staveley near Windermere. Footpaths then take you through woodland to Simpson Ground Reservoir, which although man-made is a delightful spot. The paths continue out of the forest boundary and you are greeted with views of the Leven Estuary and Whitbarrow while the distant Pennines form the skyline. A footpath takes you to

Foxfield and around Raven's Barrow, but a short diversion to the top is worth the effort for although the summit is only 155m (508ft) in altitude it provides a fine view of the valley. Descend the way you came from the summit and continue to Cartmel Fell and then cross the River Winster by road and path to Pool Bank and North Lodge.

You have now left the slate country and the west and begin to cross the limestone country of the east. A path climbs steeply through the woods and up the limestone escarpment of Whitbarrow. At the top you leave the thick woods for turf and bare limestone and are rewarded with stunning views across the valley.

Paths continue east and down through the dense woodland of The Howe and the Lyth valley. You must follow lanes out of the Lake District National Park boundary as you cross the broad, flat bottom of the valley to Brigsteer. You are now under the limestone cliffs of Scout Scar and a path can be traced along the base to Bradleyfield before climbing onto the top of the escarpment. From the top you can get a view across the whole of the Lyth valley and there is a mushroom-shaped shelter on the top where you can sit and rest a while. Of particular interest here is a painting of the view on the underside of the shelter roof. Kendal is reached by walking east across Bradleyfield on a clear path that descends to the road over the A591 Kendal bypass and into Kendal itself.

A ROUND OF WINDERMERE

Windermere is the longest lake in England, so walking all the way around its shoreline is a fitting challenge for any adventurous walker. The lake is popular with pleasure craft and the shoreline attracts tourists, bathers and picnickers, but beyond these boundaries of the lake rise wooded fells and pasture where quiet country lanes wind between sleepy hamlets and where footpaths seek out unfrequented corners and clearings that provide views across the lake to a skyline of shapely fells. This walk traces these footpaths and lanes from Newby Bridge to Ambleside to make a complete circumnavigation of Windermere with stunning views throughout.

WALK FACTS

Start/Finish	Ambleside, GR 375045
Distance	Day one: 30km (18.5 miles)
	Day two: 22.5km (14 miles)
Total ascent	Day one: 790m (2591ft)
	Day two: 400m (1312ft)
Time	Day one: 10 hours
	Day two: 7 hours

Difficulty A straightforward low-level walk but its length makes it a relatively serious undertaking. Most of the paths are clear and easily traced but some care is required to navigate through the forest areas

Accommodation Youth hostel, B&Bs, hotels and campsites around Ambleside, Newby Bridge and Windermere

Public transport Regular bus services to Ambleside and Newby Bridge with connections to the railway stations at Windermere and Kendal

DAY ONE

The tip and the toe of Windermere lake are marked by Newby Bridge and Ambleside, while Windermere and Bowness dominate the eastern shore and Grizedale Forest dominates the western shore. As this is a circular walk you could start anywhere, but this route starts from Ambleside with its more than ample provision of accommodation and facilities.

The route makes a clockwise circuit of Windermere and Wansfell Pike is your first challenge. This fell dominates Ambleside and is a popular outing for visitors to the area, even though the climb is very steep. The route leaves Ambleside by walking past the Salutation Hotel and then following the road above Stockghyll waterfall. After a cattlegrid a stile on the right gives access to the open fell which heads virtually straight up in one long slope. The views over Ambleside to the distant Coniston fells are superb, particularly early in the morning with mist lingering over the lake. But you can also see down the length of Windermere to Newby Bridge and this view includes virtually the whole route taken by this walk.

You descend east from Wansfell Pike to Troutbeck, where the cottages are stretched out in a long line rather than being gathered around a central point, to take advantage of natural springs through the valley. There's a campsite in the valley and if you walk through this you can climb to a bridleway that contours south around the flank of Applethwaite Common to Dubbs Reservoir. Lanes and field paths lead through rolling pastures to the farm at Near Orrest and then a final climb leads to Orrest Head. This is a spectacular viewpoint and a favourite with day trippers, who clamber to its rocky crown from Windermere before rapidly retreating to the comfort of a tea shop. The view includes almost all of the Lake District, with Windermere providing the foreground interest.

A clear path drops down to the busy outskirts of Windermere. To avoid the town follow the main A591 road to the left to find well-signed footpaths that lead through fields and open fell to School Knott, another fine viewpoint that is popular with the locals but little known by many visitors. You'll have to pay close attention to the map as you pick your way between lanes and field paths to Lindeth, Moor How

ALONG THE WAY

Windermere, named after a Norse hero Winand or Vinandr, is 16.9km (10.5 miles) long and 1.6km (1 mile) wide, with a maximum depth of 66m (219ft). Throughout its history it has been used as a busy highway, transporting at various times Roman troops, iron ore, charcoal and of course tourists. Regular steamer services plough through the waves to link Waterhead on the edge of Ambleside with Bowness and Newby Bridge.

Orrest Head, is a notable viewpoint that helps visitors to identify the Lake District fells as it is adorned with a view indicator. Wordsworth wrote of the view from Orrest Head:

> *Standing alone, as from a rampart's edge,*
> *I over looked the bed of Windermere,*
> *Like a vast river, stretching in the sun.*
> *With exultation, at my feet I saw*
> *Lake, islands, promontries, gleaming bays,*
> *A universe of Nature's fairest forms*
> *Proudly revealed with instantaneous burst.*

Bowness stands at the narrowest part of Lake Windermere and is the most suitable point for a ferry – a service has crossed the lake here since the fifth century. Neighbouring Windermere did not exist until the railways arrived, before this time there were only a few cottages known as Birthwaite.

Belle Island in Windermere is owned by the Curwen family who built a beautiful but unusual round house on it in 1781. The island is named after Isabella, heiress of the Curwen family.

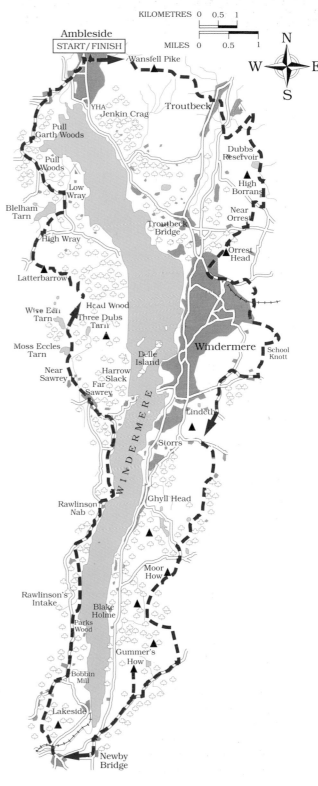

Left: View north from Gummer's How

and finally the minor road that skirts Gummer's How just north of Newby Bridge. The summit of Gummer's How is only a short walk from this road and it's well worth a visit for the view is superb and takes in the whole length of Windermere with the heart of the Lake District dominating the skyline. Newby Bridge is now only a short road walk away.

DAY TWO

To complete a full round of Windermere day two tackles the western shoreline of the lake. To escape Newby Bridge a little road walking is required over the River Leven and the line of the Lakeside and Haverthwaite Railway, where preserved steam trains can be seen in use. The road leads up the shoreline of the lake past Parks Wood, where you can leave the road for a footpath that cuts down through the trees to the water's edge. The shoreline walk doesn't last long though as you are soon back on the lane again. But this time the road walking is short-lived as a footpath can be followed to Rawlinson Nab, a finger of land that projects into Windermere to provide spectacular views both north and south across the lake.

Ambleside at the head of Windermere from Latterbarrow. Blelham Tarn is in the foreground

The path sticks with the shoreline a little longer before rejoining the road into Far Sawrey and Near Sawrey. You now enter a section of woodland walking through Claife Heights, which is part of the huge Grizedale Forest that dominates the western shore of Windermere. A bridleway leads to Moss Eccles Tarn and Wise Een Tarn fringed by trees with a superb view to the Langdale Pikes. The bridleway takes you to a crossroads, where you must turn left to descend and then climb to another crossroads. Here you turn left again and then take a footpath on the right that climbs through the woods to Latterbarrow. This is a stunning viewpoint, with vistas across Windermere to Ambleside, while the fells of central Lakeland dominate the skyline.

Descending west on a footpath from Latterbarrow you meet a minor lane which can be followed past High Wray, Blelham Tarn, Low Wray, Pull Woods and Pull Garth Woods to meet the A593 at Clappersgate with a final road walk into Ambleside.

120

CIRCUIT OF CONISTON WATER

When the high fells are shrouded in thick soupy cloud, the lower hills often provide more interesting and less challenging walking. This route encircles the lower hills around Coniston Water and you can easily escape the crowds once you climb away from the roads over fell and through forest to some of the finest and least-known viewpoints in the Lake District. The walk described begins from Spark Bridge, which allows the walker to take advantage of the wide variety of accommodation in and around Coniston village. You may actually prefer to start from the village, as bus services to Spark Bridge are very limited and irregular as they exist mainly to serve local schools.

WALK FACTS

Start/Finish Spark Bridge, GR 305849
Distance Day one: 16km (10 miles)
Day two: 19km (12 miles)
Total ascent Day one: 230m (755ft)
Day two: 350m (1148ft)
Time Day one: 5 hours
Day two: 6 hours
Difficulty Straightforward mid-level fell walking over mainly clear paths and forest tracks
Accommodation Campsites, B&Bs and youth hostels at Coniston, limited B&Bs and campsites at Spark Bridge
Public transport Regular bus services between Coniston, Ambleside and the railway station at Windermere. Very irregular bus services from Ulverston and Coniston to Spark Bridge

Peel Island in Coniston Water from Blawith Beacon

DAY ONE

Starting from Spark Bridge, your first aim is to join the Cumbria Way that runs up the west side of Coniston Water. By closely reading the map, pick your way along the bank of the River Crake to Lowick Green. Here you join the A5092 for around 300m before a path can be followed north to a church and a minor road. You then turn right and walk through Lowick. Before crossing Lowick Bridge, which spans the River Crake, take a path on the left heading gently uphill past a wood to the road near Lin Crag Farm. Follow a track from the road to the farm, and then take a path heading west to Kiln Bank -- this continues north to Tottlebank.

You have now joined the Cumbria Way, which takes you past Cockenskell to Beacon Tarn, lying in the soggy mire between the rises of Beacon Fell, Yew Bank and Coulter Stone. Twitchers may spot teal here, but at one time white-tailed eagles would have held your attention as they soared overhead.

Although Beacon Fell lies off the main Cumbria Way route, a diversion to its summit is recommended, for the view includes the Coniston Fells, Coniston Water and the Ulpha Fells, before returning to the enticing craggy outline of Dow Crag, the Old Man of Coniston and Wetherlam to the north.

From Beacon Fell the Cumbria Way strides on for the A5084 road after rounding Coats Hill, with the final leg to Coniston village following the shoreline past Torver Back Common.

DAY TWO

Leave Coniston on Tilberthwaite Avenue, heading north-west towards Hawkshead. Turn left just before the bridge over Yewdale Beck along the road

CIRCUIT OF CONISTON WATER

Coniston Fells above Coniston Water from Beacon Fell

signposted 'Ambleside'. After 200m there's a path on the right that crosses Yewdale Beck by a stone bridge. This climbs uphill and you can branch off right along a path through Guards Wood to Boom Crag Farm and the B5285 road at High Water Head.

A short road walk takes you along the B5285 road towards the lake and around its shore towards Brantwood. But from Tent Lodge, you can escape the road for a path through High Bank Ground to Low Bank Ground. You then rejoin the road from Low Bank Ground and then immediately take the bridleway through the woods that climbs south towards Lawson Park.

The route to Carron Crag takes you through Grizedale Forest Park. Plantations are often cut down and replanted, which sometimes means that forestry paths can be moved. So keep a close eye on a 1:25,000 scale map if you want to avoid getting lost.

Follow the bridleway and walk straight across the first crossroads at Lawson Park. At a large forestry road, turn left and then right at the next path junction onto a track heading south. Take the second path on the right, where the main track turns left. This leads to the summit of Carron Crag. The view from the trig point is superb, giving a full 360 degree

panorama above the surrounding forest.

To escape from Carron Crag, keep a tight grip on your map again and follow the path down the southern end of the summit crag to emerge through a gate onto a track. Turn right and then right again at the next crossroads. At the next T-junction turn left and then right after only 50m (165ft). This leads to a forestry track which you join and follow to a T-junction. Here turn left to another crossroads, where you go straight across heading south. At the next crossroads take a path on the right heading west into the trees. You soon pop out of the trees onto the lower northern slopes of Top o' Selside.

At last the navigation eases and as you contour around Top o' Selside, with a path leading up to the summit from GR 304916, your efforts are rewarded with views across Coniston Water to the high fells beyond. This a fine place to take a break.

A high-level undulating wander continues over Arnsbarrow Hill and across Bethecar Moor to High Bethecar. You now leave the open fell for farmland with clear paths taking you south through Stock to Hill Park Farm. It's now easy to link the tracks, roads and paths to Sayles Farm and the outskirts of Spark Bridge village.

ALONG THE WAY

Coniston Water is most often associated with the names of Sir Malcolm and Donald Campbell, who used the lake to achieve a world water speed record of 260.35mph in 1959. Sadly, Donald Campbell and his boat *Bluebird* ended their race against time in these waters in 1967 while attempting to break their own record. His body and the boat were never retrieved from the depths of the lake. Newspaper cuttings and photographs of the events can be studied in the Sun Hotel in Coniston.

Coniston Water is 56m (184ft) deep and 8.4km (5.2 miles) long. The lake was previously known as Thurstane Watter and was used to transport iron ore from the head of the lake to its foot. The ore was then taken to the quay at Greenodd.

The steam yacht *Gondola* was originally launched onto the lake in 1859 and lasted for eighty years running on steam power. After being taken out of service it was left to rot on the shore until the National Trust renovated it and brought it back into service in 1980. Today it once again provides a unique method of touring the lake, as it is the only steam-powered yacht in the Lake District.

Coniston Water has many literary links. In Arthur Ransome's *Swallows and Amazons* stories, Peel Island was featured as Wild Cat Island. Alfred Tennyson (1809–92), the poet Laureate in 1850, spent his honeymoon at Tent Lodge on the east shore, while John Ruskin lived at Brantwood from 1871 until his death in 1900.

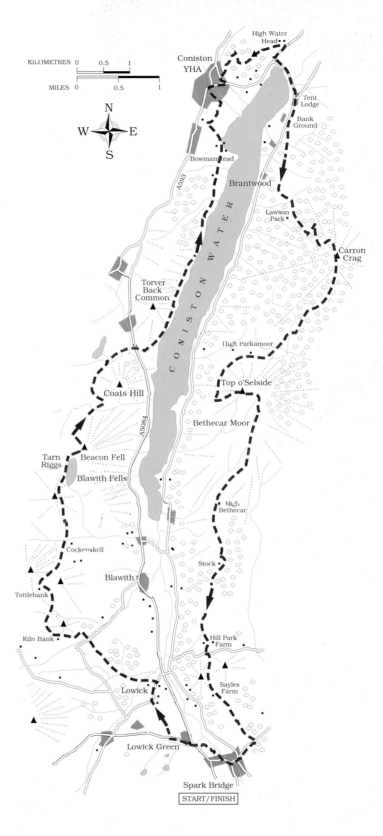

NEWBY BRIDGE TO HAWKSHEAD

The western shoreline of Windermere is dominated by the low wooded hills of Grizedale Forest, which were originally planted to provide charcoal for the iron furnaces of south Lakeland and to be used for the manufacture of bobbins and baskets. The forest was also the first Forestry Commission estate to provide information for walkers and visitors so that today the area has a number of marked trails and an unusual exhibition of woodland sculptures. Walks in this area combine views and a shoreline traverse of England's largest lake, visits to idyllic tarns, huge forests and pretty hamlets with surprise views at clearings and exposed summits. But above all, this is Beatrix Potter country, for the famous author of the Peter Rabbit books lived at Near Sawrey and now her former home, Hill Top, is a world-famous tourist attraction.

DAY ONE

To arrive in style at Newby Bridge you could take a ferry down the length of Windermere from either Waterhead near Ambleside or Bowness. Once here you are set for a fine walk along the western shore of the lake before heading for the woods to Hawkshead. To begin you must follow roads, but they are quiet in this southern tip of the Lake District. The roads lead around Lakeside, where the Windermere ferry pulls into port and then to the Stott Park Bobbin Mill, a working museum of traditional Lakeland crafts such as the making of bobbins for the Lancashire cotton industry.

Road walking continues along the lake shore passing the YMCA National Centre for outdoor pursuits along the way. Then you can take a footpath that cuts down through the trees to the water's edge for views across the lake to the steamers and pleasure craft that are always present on Windermere. The shoreline walk doesn't last long and soon you are back on the lane again. You can escape once more though, this time to a path that leads to Rawlinson Nab, a finger of land that projects into Windermere to provide an outstanding view north over the lake to Red Screes, Caudale Moor, Troutbeck, High Street, Froswick and Ill Bell in the Eastern Fells.

The path sticks with the shoreline a little longer before rejoining the road into Far Sawrey and Near Sawrey. An enclosed bridleway takes you through the forests to Moss Eccles Tarn and Wise Een Tarn. The views from here extend beyond the forest to the famous fists of the Langdale Pikes. The bridleway continues to a crossroads, where you must turn left to descend and then climb to another crossroads. Here you turn left again and then take a footpath on the right that climbs through the woods to Latterbarrow. This is a marvellous viewpoint that includes virtually a complete panorama of the Lakeland fells. Descending west on a footpath from Latterbarrow you meet a minor lane and a series of footpaths can then be linked to take you to Hawkshead.

WALK FACTS

Start/Finish	Newby Bridge, GR 370860
Distance	Day one: 16km (10 miles)
	Day two: 16km (10 miles)
Total ascent	Day one: 300m (984ft)
	Day two: 400m (1312ft)
Time	Day one: 6 hours
	Day two: 6 hours

Difficulty A straightforward low-level walk through forests and along the lake shore, where navigation can be tricky through the wooded sections
Accommodation Youth hostel, B&Bs, hotels and campsites around Hawkshead with limited B&B accommodation at Newby Bridge
Public transport Regular bus services to Hawkshead and Newby Bridge with connections to the railway stations at Windermere and Kendal

ALONG THE WAY

Grizedale Forest is a working production forest but also home to a unique sculpture project established in 1977 to provide a working environment for sculptures. The sculptures are scattered through the forest and they range from giant woodmen to musical instruments and tiny animals.

Stott Park Bobbin Mill was opened in 1835 to produce bobbins for the Lancashire cotton factories. The raw materials of the bobbins came from the coppice woods of Grizedale forest while power was provided by damming Finsthwaite Tarn. The water from the tarn flowed downhill to drive a 9.7m (32ft) water-wheel which powered the mill machinery. In 1858 a water turbine replaced the wheel and this required constant pressure, so a second dam was built. Today these dams are called High Dam and Low Dam and they sit on the hill above the bobbin mill. The mill was closed in 1971 but later reopened as a working museum where traditional woodland crafts such as the production of bobbins, baskets, barrel hoops and staves for ships can be seen. Oak bark was also used to tan leather and much of the forests were used to produce charcoal to fire the furnaces of Southern Lakeland.

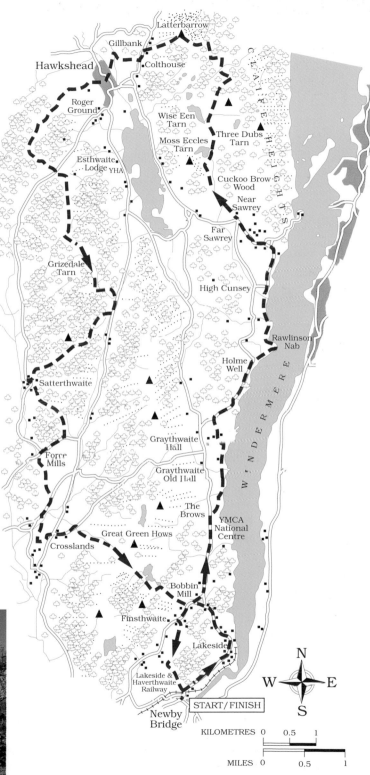

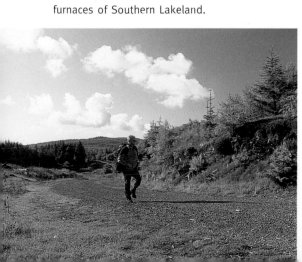

125

NEWBY BRIDGE TO HAWKSHEAD

Below: The southern end of Windermere from Gummers How

DAY TWO

It wasn't until the nineteenth century that roads extended to Hawkshead, but today it is busy with tourists who come to walk its maze of narrow streets, visit Wordsworth's old school and see an exhibition of Beatrix Potter's original Peter Rabbit illustrations.

You can escape the busy village quite easily, however, by walking west past the fifteenth century church that sits on a knoll. This path provides fine views over Hawkshead and takes you between fields up onto Hawkshead Moor, where you enter the woods once again. Your route stays high, with the footpath passing a tarn before swinging south-east to the minor road that links Hawkshead with Grizedale. Walk straight across the road to re-enter the woods and follow a footpath in a southerly direction.

This part of the walk passes a number of woodland sculptures with a large gathering of them around Grizedale Tarn and on the route down to the road at High Dale Park. This unique open-air gallery was started in 1977 and in 1990 it won the Prudential Award for Arts. Shortly after joining the road at Dale Park, you leave it again for a bridleway that leads south-west up steep slopes to a fine viewpoint over Dale Park, which was originally designed as a deer hunting area in 1516. Deer are still common in the area so keep a look-out as you descend past more wood sculptures into Satterthwaite. In particular look out for a short diversion to Wild Boar Clearing, one of the most outstanding sculptures in the forest.

A bridleway leaves Satterthwaite for Low Dale Park where you need to walk along the lane to Force Mills. A footpath cuts through the fields to Thwaite Head and then it's a road walk before you can use a path to reach Crosslands. The final climb of the day takes you up a footpath from Crosslands past Great Green Hows to High Dam, a National Trust area that was built to serve the bobbin mills but now rests in beautiful isolation along the pine-clad shore. A clear path takes you down to Finsthwaite, with a final walk along a footpath returning you to Newby Bridge.

BROUGHTON IN FURNESS TO CONISTON

This walk makes a traverse of the Dunnerdale and Furness Fells, linking Broughton in Furness with Coniston. Think of Coniston and you'll think of the great range of fells that tower above the village including the Old Man of Coniston, Wetherlam, Dow Crag and Swirl How, while the neighbouring peaks of the Dunnerdale and Furness Fells are hardly given a thought. Yet these lesser-known fells have much to offer those in search of relatively untamed fells where walkers can immerse themselves in the search for solitude and discover a whole new area of the Lake District in the process. The area is almost like a miniature Lakeland with idyllic tarns, steep crags, sweeping valleys and shapely peaks that barely reach the 2000ft contour, while most struggle to even gain 1000ft.

DAY ONE

This walk starts at Broughton in Furness to make use of the ample accommodation at Coniston for the overnight stay. If you are relying on public transport you might prefer to begin from Coniston village, as bus services to Broughton in Furness are limited, though this will mean you have less choice for accommodation around Broughton in Furness.

From the centre of Broughton in Furness a walled lane takes you over the remains of the Broughton in Furness to Coniston railway, which was closed in 1958. A waymarked route runs parallel with the railway through fields to Wall End Farm. But before reaching the farm a waymarked path on the right

Wetherlam from Blawith Beacon

WALK FACTS

Start/Finish	Broughton in Furness, GR 212875
Distance	Day one: 17.7km (11 miles)
	Day two: 21km (13 miles)
Total ascent	Day one: 300m (984ft)
	Day two: 980m (3215ft)
Time	Day one: 5 hours
	Day two: 7 hours

Difficulty Medium-level fell walking where care is required finding your way over the fells which are seldom walked and have few paths

Accommodation Campsites, B&Bs and youth hostels at Coniston, limited B&Bs in Broughton in Furness

Public transport Regular bus services between Coniston, Ambleside and the railway station at Windermere. Very irregular bus services to Broughton in Furness

BROUGHTON IN FURNESS TO CONISTON

*Below: Snow-covered Coniston Fells from
Blawith Beacon*

takes you down to a lane, which is crossed to follow a woodland track to a road. Turn left here to pick up a path on the right that leads across the valley to Thornthwaite Latter Rigg. The summit brings splendid views of the neighbouring hills and dales and is an early highlight of the walk.

Clear tracks continue to Woodland Hall Farm and a moorland road where you turn left for around 500m and then right along a signposted bridleway that leads over the moors to Spunham Farm and Green Moor Farm. The bridleway climbs around the northern edge of Blawith Knott (pronounced Blaith Knott) to a col. The path then begins to descend towards Cockenskell. Look out for a crossroads of paths here as this is where you join the Cumbria Way long-distance path which takes you to Beacon Tarn. Birdwatchers may see teal here, but at one time they might have seen white-tailed eagles soaring overhead. A diversion to Beacon Fell brings outstanding views down the length of Coniston Water to the distant

peaks, making this an exceptional yet little-known viewpoint.

The end of the day sees you following the Cumbria Way to the A5084 road which is crossed for a shoreline walk through Torver Back Common and on to Coniston village.

DAY TWO

The Walna Scar Road is more of a rough track than a road and it has been used for centuries as a trade route to link Coniston with Dunnerdale and Eskdale. Today it provides a useful route for walkers wishing to pass between the two valleys or climb on the fells. The road begins with a steep climb outside the Sun Hotel in Coniston, a popular walkers' haunt. It then climbs steadily until it reaches a gate on the edge of the open fell. Many walkers drive to this point, leaving their cars in the car park before tackling the heights of Dow Crag and the Old Man of Coniston.

The Walna Scar Road continues as a rough track

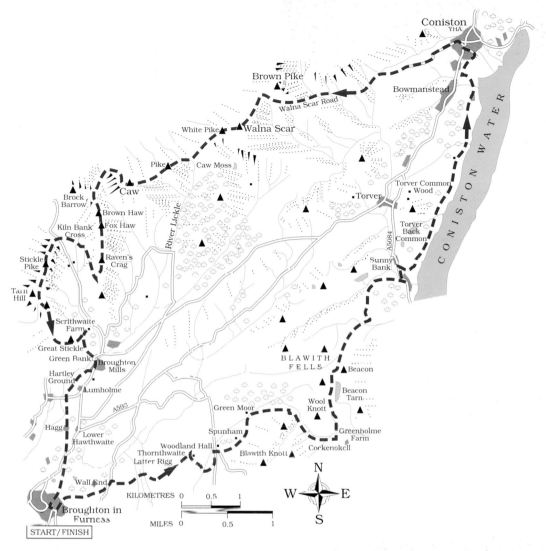

ALONG THE WAY

The **Woodland Fells** between Broughton in Furness and Coniston Water is an area of ragged Silurian slate where rocky outcrops burst from gorse, juniper, heather and bilberry. The area is criss-crossed with footpaths and unfenced roads and Wainwright described a walk in this area as, 'a connoisseur's piece, every step an uninhibited joy, every corner a delight'.

Broughton in Furness is a small village with a spacious market place built around an obelisk. In about 1760 John Gilpin Sawrey, the Lord of the Manor, laid out the design for the square and asked local craftsmen to build the terraces of houses. Sawrey used the Manor Arms Hotel (known as the King's Head at that time) as his office while selling off the buildings. The Town Hall was already in existence at this time so this was incorporated into the design of the square, with the clock being added to the façade in 1766. The Town Hall was given to the people of Broughton in 1947, when Sir Robert Rankin gave up the lordship of the area to Lancashire County Council.

The obelisk in the middle of the square in Broughton was erected in 1810 as a gift from Mrs Gilpin to commemorate the 50th year of the reign of King George III. In 1859 the **railway** around the coast of Cumbria that linked Broughton to Carlisle and Lancaster was extended to Coniston. This made it possible to transport copper ore from the mines at Coniston more easily, without having to use boats and horse-drawn carts. But the decline and eventual closure of the Coniston mines meant that the railway was mostly dependent on tourist traffic by 1900 and by 1957 the branch-line to Coniston was closed as it was uneconomic.

Below: Snow on Red Screes above Ambleside and Coniston Water from Blawith Beacon

now, climbing around the lower slopes of the Old Man of Coniston, with splendid views over Coniston Water and the Furness and Dunnerdale Fells to the left. At its highest point the Walna Scar Road touches the base of Brown Pike before dropping into Dunnerdale. Most walkers head for Brown Pike and Dow Crag from here, but on this walk you turn your back on these fells for the less popular and less well-trodden Dunnerdale Fells.

A faint path leads the way across Walna Scar with outstanding views to the Scafell massif to the north. The summit cairn of White Pike is a particularly fine viewpoint, with the ground sweeping down steeply from below your feet. To the south of White Pike a bridleway can be seen descending down the side of the woods and along the banks of the River Lickle. Although this looks tempting it's best to stay high and instead pick your own route over the soggy mire of Caw Moss before climbing steadily west over the broad shoulder of Pike. Follow the ridge to Caw with its trig point that provides a splendid view of the Duddon valley. The rocky crown of Brock Barrow is your next objective, but to reach it you must first descend north-west to reach an abandoned mine level, which can be followed to the left to reach a track that

crosses Long Mire Beck. If you follow the track alongside the wall you can then climb a stone stile to reach the summit of Brock Barrow, where you get more fine views down into the Duddon valley.

You have to return back the way you came before you can climb south to the summit of Fox Haw, with its squat cairn sitting astride a narrow summit rock. Further to the south rises Raven's Crag at 361m (1184ft) and then you descend south to reach a bridleway which can be traced to Kiln Bank Cross, the highest point of a road pass linking Broughton Mills with the Duddon valley. By walking straight across the road you can climb past Stickle Tarn to Stickle Pike, with its cairn marking a fine panoramic view that includes Pillar, Scafell, Bowfell, the Coniston fells, Black Combe and the Duddon Estuary.

Walking south, you pass the tarns of Tarn Hill before gaining the summit of Great Stickle where there's a trig point, even though this isn't the highest point on these fells. To end the walk you descend west around the base of Great Stickle past Scrithwaite Farm, Green Bank Farm and onto a road that crosses the River Lickle and enters Broughton Mills only a short path and road walk from Broughton in Furness.

SPARK BRIDGE TO HAWKSHEAD

The huge Grizedale Forest dominates the low hills that rise between Coniston Water and Windermere. The forest has been used to provide raw materials for local industry for centuries and to this day it is still a working forest. It is also home to a unique collection of woodland sculptures and you never quite know what will appear as you turn a corner as the forest is quite literally littered with wood sculptures of animals, giants, musical instruments and unusual shelters. When you escape the forests you get extensive views across much of Southern Lakeland with the ever-present skyline of the mighty central fells dominating the views to the north. This walk makes a circular traverse of this area, linking the villages of Spark Bridge and Hawkshead.

Wood carving on Carron Crag

WALK FACTS

Start/Finish Spark Bridge, GR 305849
Distance Day one: 19km (12 miles)
Day two: 19km (12 miles)
Total ascent Day one: 300m (984ft)
Day two: 400m (1312ft)
Time Day one: 7 hours
Day two: 7 hours
Difficulty Straightforward mid-level fell walking along country lanes and through forests where some careful navigation is required to trace paths
Accommodation Campsites, B&Bs and youth hostels at Hawkshead, limited B&Bs and campsites at Spark Bridge
Public transport Regular bus services between Hawkshead, Ambleside and the railway station at Windermere. Very irregular bus services from Ulverston and Coniston to Spark Bridge

DAY ONE

The walk begins from Spark Bridge, which allows the walker to take advantage of the wide variety of accommodation in and around Hawkshead village. If you are relying on public transport you may prefer to start from Hawkshead, as bus services to Spark Bridge are very limited.

The first half of the day links quiet lanes with field paths and the walking begins with a steep climb out of Spark Bridge on the road to Colton. A footpath continues around the outskirts of Oxen Park and then it's back to road walking to Hulleter. Another footpath takes you down over Rusland Pool to Rusland itself. You have to use the road once more to carry you north to where a footpath climbs through the woods to Force Mills.

The Grizedale Forest section now begins with a short road walk to the right before you can climb through the forest to Satterthwaite. An ancient

Opposite: Grizedale Tarn

ALONG THE WAY

There are many tiny villages and country houses in the area to the east of Spark Bridge. **Booth** is the largest village but nearby **Colton** was the administrative centre until recently. Colton church stands on the hillside removed from the village. It is larger than many country churches as it served a large parish. The church includes the Dickson memorial window, featuring local birds and flowers.

Hawkshead is a market town and even though it is one of the smallest towns in the country it has a town hall. The name means Haukr's sheiling or summer meadow, Haukr being a Norse personal name. Until recently it was well off the beaten track and largely self-sufficient. It was originally established as a centre for the local wool and timber industries and traders brought goods to the market by packhorse from all over Lakeland.

   Today Hawkshead is famous for its grammar school where William Wordsworth inscribed his name on his desk while studying there between 1779 and 1787. There's also a Beatrix Potter Gallery in Hawkshead which has a collection of over 500 of Beatrix Potter's original watercolours and drawings which were used in her Peter Rabbit series of books.

Carron Crag, although surrounded by forest, has been left exposed above the tree tops to provide an unrivalled 360 degree view of Southern Lakeland with the skyline to the west, north and east dominated by the higher fells of Lakeland.

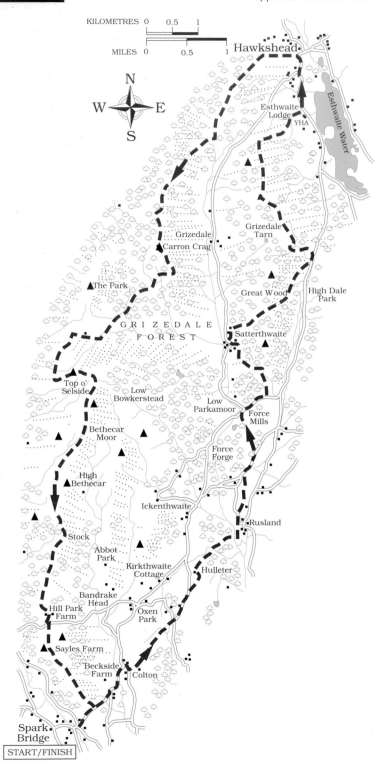

bridleway crosses the forest from Satterthwaite to the Windermere ferry from Sawrey to Bowness. This is your route and it brings you face to face with the first of many woodland sculptures. It lies just off the path as you climb out of Satterthwaite and is called 'Wild Boar Clearing' and it is regarded by many as one of the finest works of art in the forest. Later you'll also see a sculpture entitled 'Axis of the Earth' by a Japanese artist Masao Ueno.

Blue markers guide you along the correct tracks that lead through Great Wood to the road just north of High Dale Park. This area was once created for deer hunting and today you'll see plenty of deer in the woods. Join the road and follow it north before escaping to the woods again on a bridleway that climbs north-west towards Grizedale Tarn and then north to escape the forests and reveal views over Hawkshead and Esthwaite Water. The lake can be reached by descending a path that leads into the back of Esthwaite Lodge which is today used as Hawkshead Youth Hostel. This is a fine place to stay overlooking the lake, while Hawkshead village is only a short road walk away.

DAY TWO

Hawkshead is popular with tourists, but if you wish you can quickly escape the busy streets by walking out towards the village church which stands on a small knoll, with fine views over Hawkshead.

The path climbs through the woods once more as

you again return to the sculptures of Grizedale Forest. The path soon meets a forest track and bridleway which can be followed steadily uphill in a south-westerly direction. You are heading for the summit of Carron Crag, and soon you join a waymarked path called the Silurian Way, which makes a circuit of the forest from the Grizedale Visitor Centre. The forest track passes the Hollow Spruce sculpture and Pyxis sculptures and then you can enter a deer gate on the left with a path climbing to Carron Crag. The summit remains unplanted and you are rewarded with a fine panoramic view. There used to be a hut on the summit, anchored to the ground with guy lines, but this has recently been removed.

To descend, walk over the summit following poles through bracken to meet a forest track once more. Here you turn right and then right again to follow a track south-west. You need to continue in this direction until you emerge from the forest. You will then join a track that contours around the open fell of Top o' Selside. A path leaves the track to the west of the summit and climbs directly to the top revealing another superb viewpoint, taking in Coniston Water and the Coniston Fells.

Walk straight over Top o' Selside and then turn south on a footpath that descends from the open fell to High Bethecar and the lanes at Stock. All that remains is to walk along a bridleway through Hill Park Farm and Sayles Farm to emerge on the road just outside Spark Bridge.

Opposite: Little Langdale with Great Carrs behind

PENRITH TO RAVENGLASS VIA AMBLESIDE

When the Romans came to Britain they built forts throughout Cumbria to protect their advance across the land. In particular there were forts at Penrith, Ambleside, Eskdale and Ravenglass, a busy port in those days. So that the Roman legions could travel across the densely forested country they built roads and these often followed straight lines across the highest land, to provide a direct link between locations and also to avoid the valleys where ambushes were a continual threat. The most famous Roman road in Cumbria linked the fort at Penrith with their fort at Ambleside and crossed the High Street range of fells. More detective work shows proof of a route linking the Ambleside fort with Eskdale and finally Ravenglass on the west coast.

DAY ONE

The walk begins from Penrith and although the course of the original Roman road is unclear here, as is the location of the Roman fort, there is evidence of the route on the outskirts of the town. The modern walker must do battle with the M6 motorway at Junction 40 from where a short walk along the A66 towards Keswick provides access to a path that leads through the woods, under the railway line, past Redhills to cross the River Eamont and climb to Sockbridge and Tirril. This is farmland with limited rights-of-way, so you need to follow roads and lanes to Celleron and Winder Hall Farm.

At last you can leave the roads for a bridleway that continues from the farm around Heughscar Hill to a path junction above Roehead. The clear fells lie ahead and you are now on the course of the Roman road

WALK FACTS

Start	Penrith, GR 511300
Finish	Ravenglass, GR 805965
Distance	Day one: 33.7km (21 miles)
	Day two: 33.7km (21 miles)
Total ascent	Day one: 1060m (3478ft)
	Day two: 850m (2789ft)
Time	Day one: 11 hours
	Day two: 10 hours

Difficulty A very long walk over high fells and a valley route following clear paths with some road walking. As the route is so long it may be split into shorter sections over three or four days

Accommodation B&Bs, hotels and campsites at Penrith, Patterdale, Ambleside, Troutbeck, Eskdale, Ravenglass, with youth hostels at Patterdale, Ambleside, Troutbeck and Eskdale

Public transport Penrith and Ravenglass have railway stations and Ambleside is linked to Windermere railway station by a bus service. The only public transport in Eskdale is the Ravenglass and Eskdale Railway which extends from Ravenglass to Dalegarth Station. Ravenglass has connections to the west coast main line

that climbs south onto Barton Fell bound for Loadpot Hill and onto High Street. The path continues in a generally south-south-westerly direction and traverses the high fells that would have risen above the tree-line back in Roman times, while the valleys would have been almost impassable due to the dense woodland and undergrowth. The walking is easy these days over High Street, but no doubt it would have been somewhat harder for the Romans with their poor outdoor equipment and footwear.

The main path descends around the head of Haweswater and then climbs to Thornthwaite Crag, where you will enjoy views down the length of Windermere. The course of the Roman road becomes uncertain once more. Some say the route followed a high-level course over Froswick, Ill Bell and Yoke, while there is also a chance that the route went down Scot Rake, leaving the ridge just north of Froswick. This walk follows the Scot Rake alternative, descending

PENRITH TO RAVENGLASS VIA AMBLESIDE

Opposite: Thornthwaite Crag summit cairn with
Windermere in the distance

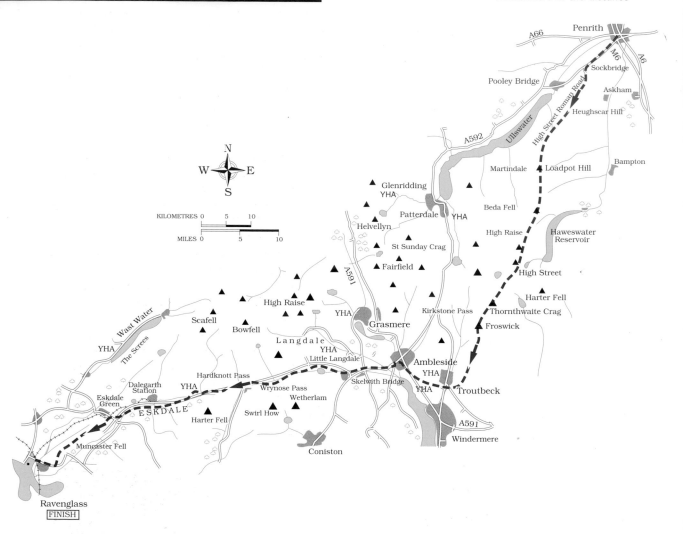

ALONG THE WAY

The history of the **Roman occupation of Cumbria** is complicated and unclear, but between AD84 and AD120 the Romans established a chain of forts in Cumbria with a series of roads linking each fort to its neighbour. The Roman army remained in Cumbria for over 300 years, making its final withdrawal in AD383, but leaving these clear marks of their occupation.

Around Penrith the Roman fort was situated to the east of the town and a fort platform can be seen south of the A6 and River Eamont (GR 538288). The Galava fort can be seen in Borran's Field at Waterhead on the shores of Windermere. The foundations are visible on the ground and finds from the site can be seen in the Armitt Museum in Ambleside. Hardknott fort is the best-preserved Roman fort outside of Hadrian's wall. It stands in a spectacular

position, with magnificent views down Eskdale to the west. The fort was built between AD117 and AD138 to hold a garrison of 500 and the Roman soldiers no doubt greeted their arrival at the fort with its bath-house with great relief after their 16km (10 mile) march from Ambleside. At Ravenglass there is Walls Castle, which was a bath-house attached to the original Roman fort that has now been destroyed by the construction of the railway.

steadily down the broad path to Limefitt Park.

You can end the day here or in the nearby Windermere youth hostel. But if you have the energy, keep walking to Ambleside from Troutbeck via Robin Lane and the fine viewpoint of Jenkin's Crag, before finally emerging onto the road at Ambleside, where you can visit the remains of the Roman Galava fort.

DAY TWO

There's little trace of the Roman road through Ambleside and the nearest we can get to it is to follow the A593 Coniston Road to Clappersgate, where the B5286 Hawkshead road can be followed on the left to Skelwith Fold. If you turn right here, you'll arrive at Skelwith Bridge, from where the Cumbria Way can be followed through woods to Park Farm, Low Park and finally Colwith Force waterfall. The path leaves the waterfall and emerges from the wood onto a lane at High Park. The Cumbria Way turns left here, but you should turn right and follow the lane to Stang End. Keep following the main track as it leads between the high fells and Little Langdale valley, passing to the south of Little Langdale Tarn. Take a right fork to Bridge End until finally you arrive at Fell Foot Bridge, where the Wrynose Pass road is joined and you are at last back on the tracks of the Romans.

The road over the Wrynose Pass closely follows the course of the original Roman road, with its steep zigzags conquering the 40 per cent incline of the pass. From the top of the pass the original route becomes clearer still as it traces the bank of the River Duddon through Wrynose Bottom. Today you can walk down the valley by using a footpath to the north of the river, and at Cockley Bridge a clear track leads to Black Hall along the original course of the Roman road. The route follows zigzags up the edge of the plantation to the summit of Hardknott Pass, with stunning views into both Eskdale and Wrynose Bottom.

A short descent from Hardknott Pass leads to the remains of Hardknott Roman Fort, where the Roman legions took a well-earned rest after their march from Ambleside. The Roman road becomes unclear through Eskdale and today the best route through the valley is along the banks of the River Esk. This carries you through Penny Hill Farm and Low Birker to the outflow of Stanley Gill waterfall. A short diversion up the gorge brings views of a spectacular cascade of water forced through a narrow rock crevice.

Stay with the River Esk as far as the road at Forge Bridge and then walk along the southern base of Muncaster Fell or take the path over the fell itself, finally descending down Fell Lane, a route that was used by the Romans. Ravenglass and the remains of Walls Castle, a Roman bath-house, are well within a final march for both the Romans and the modern-day backpacker.

Opposite: Froswick, Ill Bell and Yoke from the High Street plateau

WINDERMERE TO PENRITH VIA SHAP

The far eastern fringe of the Lake District is possibly the quietest corner of the National Park as the area is largely bypassed by walkers and tourists. There are no real tourist centres, no valleys dedicated to climbing and no special mountains, but this lack doesn't mean that there is nothing to discover. In fact the eastern fringe of the Lake District is a unique quarter. Here, long-remote dales slip between low-lying fells. Paths are few, space is everywhere and solitude is easy to find. The walker who ventures into this part of the Lake District will find it more of a wilderness experience than the central fells could ever hope to offer. This walk makes a grand traverse of Lakeland's eastern fringe and links the railway stations at Windermere and Penrith in the process.

DAY ONE

From Windermere your first climb leads up to Orrest Head, one of the finest viewpoints in the Lake District, which extends across the Lake District to the Howgill and Pennine mountains. The fells stretch out to the east but you have to wind your way through fields and lanes before you can climb them. Paths lead through meadows to the farms at Near Orrest and Moor Howe. The Dubbs Road takes you past Dubbs Reservoir and finally you join the Garburn Pass above Troutbeck. This old packhorse route provides easy walking today, as it has done over the centuries, with wonderful views across the Troutbeck valley to Wansfell.

At the highest point of the Garburn Pass turn left for the ascent of the Yoke, Ill Bell and Froswick trio of hills that form a superb roller-coaster ridge. At Thornthwaite Crag the main path descends around the head of Hayeswater Gill before rising onto the great mound of High Street. The large, rounded plateau means that views from High Street are a little disappointing when compared with those elsewhere in the range. But High Street is the highest hill in the eastern fells and at one time formed part of a Roman road that linked the forts at Penrith with those around Ambleside and Windermere.

After a lunch break on High Street descend south-east over Mardale Ill Bell to the Nan Bield Pass, with its extensive views north over Small Water and Haweswater Reservoir. A punishingly steep climb leads up onto Harter Fell, with its strange summit cairn comprised of fence posts and rock. The tone of the walk changes a little now as you leave the high fells for a low valley walk.

Walk from Harter Fell to Gatesgarth Pass and then descend south-east towards Longsleddale. Keep your eyes open for a signpost marking a bridleway heading east-north-east for Swindale Head and Stack Howe. The path isn't clear and crosses a soggy mire before rising steadily up to Mosedale Cottage. Thankfully a clear path appears here and this is followed towards Swindale Head. But things aren't that easy on this walk, as you need to leave the path again to cross Mosedale Beck and climb up and over

WALK FACTS

Start	Windermere, GR 415985
Finish	Penrith, GR 515305
Distance	Day one: 29km (18 miles)
	Day two: 19km (12 miles)
Total ascent	Day one: 1040m (3412ft)
	Day two: 100m (328ft)
Time	Day one: 9 hours
	Day two: 5 hours

Difficulty Straightforward walking on clear paths over high fells with a low-level section on day two. There are no obvious alternative routes and day one is very long

Accommodation Campsites at Windermere and Shap, youth hostel at Windermere, B&Bs and hotels at Windermere, Shap and Penrith

Public transport Railway stations at Penrith and Windermere; bus services link Penrith to Shap

WINDERMERE TO PENRITH VIA SHAP

ALONG THE WAY

Shap was once at the centre of a thriving agricultural economy and a market was established there in 1687. This was given a boost by the arrival of the railway in the mid-nineteenth century as it allowed Westmorland butter to be transported from Shap to London each week. The local blue and pink granite was also transported throughout the country. The wealthy flocked to the sulphur well at Shap to 'take its waters', which were thought able to cure just about anything. Today Shap is bypassed by the M6 and passenger rail services do not stop here. During the backpacking season, however, walkers pass through the village as they leave the Lake District for the Yorkshire Dales on Wainwright's Coast-to-Coast path.

Work began on the building of Shap Abbey in the twelfth century but additions were still being made up until the sixteenth century. In 1540 the building was surrendered to Henry VIII and soon fell into disrepair. Today only the west tower remains and it is preserved as an ancient monument by English Heritage.

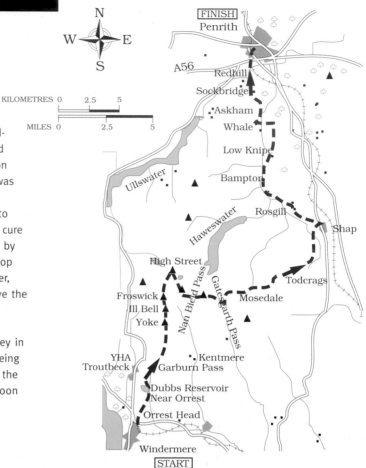

the moor into Wet Sleddale. As you descend into the valley, you'll soon pick up a path that makes a descending traverse of the hillside towards Wet Sleddale Reservoir. A track leads through Sleddale Hall, Sleddale Grange, Bowfield and across the fields to Steps Hall. A final road walk takes you into Shap.

DAY TWO

A change is as good as a rest and the walk to Penrith is very different from the one from Windermere. The high fells and lonely valleys of day one are replaced with quiet rolling countryside where field paths link small villages that lie scattered over this far north-eastern corner of the Lake District.

Leave Shap by following signs for 'Bampton, Haweswater and Shap Abbey'. These direct you down a lane to the Abbey, the River Lowther and the boundary of the Lake District National Park. You are now in the countryside with cattle and sheep roaming the fields through which paths continue along the banks of the River Lowther to the attractive houses at Rosgill. You soon return to the banks of the river and arrive at Bampton Grange via a kissing gate beside the church. Turn left to cross the river and then turn right. The road leads over Haweswater Beck and then

Above: Hiker on Harter Fell – Haweswater in the distance
Opposite: Blea Water with High Street on the left

a footpath can be taken on the right that once more follows the river bank.

It's a delightful river-bank walk to Low Knipe where you must join the road to Whale and Whale Farm. A path leads north alongside a wood to return you to the banks of the River Lowther with opportunities to spot herons, oystercatchers, curlews and lapwings. Finally, the path veers away from the river as you head through woods towards Askham Church and Askham Bridge, which you use to cross the River Lowther once again.

The main street of Askham is lined with fine cottages set well back from the road. If you fancy a break, stop at the Queen's Head Inn which dates from the seventeenth century when Askham was on the main trade route from Pooley Bridge to the markets at Appleby. Road walking takes you past Barnet Wood to Lowclose, where paths lead to Tirril and Sockbridge and signposts direct you to the A66 at Junction 40 on the outskirts of Penrith.

SHAP TO RAVENGLASS VIA GRASMERE

One of the great challenges of Lakeland walking is a side-to-side crossing of the district from Shap to Ravenglass. Heading west from Shap the walker enters a land that is almost Pennine in shape and form, but gradually the crags break through and the hills begin to climb steeper into the sky as the eastern fells take on their true identity at the head of Haweswater. The great spine of High Street is crossed and the fells develop further as you leave the rolling hills and enter the Ullswater valley with Helvellyn's rocky ridges rising ahead. You then conquer the heart of Lakeland via High Raise, bypassing Scafell Pike for remote Eskdale,

WALK FACTS

Start	Shap, GR 564153
Finish	Ravenglass, GR 085965
Distance	Day one: 33.7km (21 miles)
	Day two: 33.7km (21 miles)
Total ascent	Day one: 1050m (3445ft)
	Day two: 900m (2953ft)
Time	Day one: 10 hours
	Day two: 10 hours

Difficulty A very long walk over mountain paths that require the long daylight hours of summer if it is to be completed in two days

Accommodation B&Bs, campsites and hotels at Ravenglass, Grasmere and Shap; youth hostels at Grasmere

Public transport Ravenglass is served by a railway as well as various bus services. Ravenglass and Eskdale are linked by a rail service. Bus services link Shap with Kendal and Penrith and also link Grasmere with the railway station at Windermere

where once more the mountains reduce in height and become more rolling as you end the journey in the coastal town of Ravenglass.

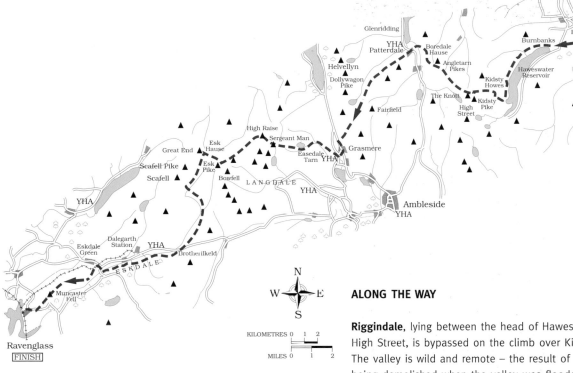

ALONG THE WAY

Riggindale, lying between the head of Haweswater and High Street, is bypassed on the climb over Kidsty Pike. The valley is wild and remote – the result of the area being demolished when the valley was flooded to create the reservoir. Today Riggindale is home to deer, fell ponies, foxes and golden eagles.

The **Grisedale valley** between Patterdale and Grasmere has been used for centuries by local people but was also adopted as the fashionable route onto Helvellyn when the ascent was often made on the backs of ponies in the eighteenth century.

A short distance below Grisedale Tarn is a boulder known as Brother's Parting. It was here that William Wordsworth said a last farewell to his brother John in 1805. Shortly after this John was tragically drowned in the ship that he commanded.

The **Upper Eskdale valley i**s surrounded by a cirque of mountains including Scafell, Scafell Pike, Esk Pike, Bowfell and Crinkle Crags. The valley provides an easier route through the mountains than tackling the high fells. It also provides, arguably, the finest views of Scafell Pike, the southern face of which is intricately formed into folds, cliffs and knobs of rock, with slivers of water slipping down between the shapely rocks.

Left: Sourmilk Gill, Easedale
Opposite: Sunrise from Grisedale Tarn

DAY ONE

As the walk is 67km (42 miles) long, it takes the easiest line through the mountains, often following a gentle valley path instead of a high mountain route. Some tough hikers have been known to walk this distance in a long eighteen-hour summer day! But with so many choices of accommodation, the route could also be split into a three- or four-day expedition or you could add in extra peaks to make the trip tougher!

There's a bus service to Shap from Penrith and plenty of accommodation to allow an early start on day one. This first day follows the Coast-to-Coast route in reverse from Shap as far as Grasmere. So leave Shap by following signs for the ruined Shap Abbey and then follow field paths north-west alongside the River Lowther to Rosgill Bridge and Rawhead. Your route traverses the banks of Haweswater Reservoir which hides the submerged village of Mardale Green, although in dry summers you can sometimes still see stone walls and even a bridge at the head of the reservoir exposed to the air once more.

The path leads into Riggindale, a popular place to find twitchers who are hoping to see England's only pair of golden eagles, which live high on the crags. You now climb up to Kidsty Howes and Kidsty Pike, with superb views over Haweswater Reservoir and across to High Street, the highest point of these eastern fells. The main track bypasses the summit of High Street by around 2km, but as you are so close it wouldn't add too much to your overall journey to take in the summit.

It's now a long, steady descent around The Knott and past Angle Tarn to Boredale Hause. At times the path winds an intricate line close to the steepest slopes, making this a wonderful section of the walk, giving spectacular views down into Ullswater and across the valley to the Helvellyn range.

Having dipped into Patterdale in the Ullswater valley, the mountain barrier of Helvellyn, Fairfield and St Sunday Crag rise up ahead. As you've already come a long way today, the easiest route through the mountain barrier is the Grisedale valley. This takes you between St Sunday Crag and Striding Edge and up to Grisedale Tarn from where an easy descent brings a welcome rest in Grasmere.

SHAP TO RAVENGLASS VIA GRASMERE

Below: Walking towards Scafell Pike across Great Moss, Upper Eskdale

DAY TWO

You now leave Wainwright's Coast-to-Coast route as you head for Easedale Tarn, via the milky waterfall of Sourmilk Gill. This was one of William Wordsworth's favourite walks and today tourists flock to tread in his footsteps in search of poetic understanding.

Climb steadily on a fainter path towards Belles Knott. The pyramidal shape of the peak looks quite impressive as you climb but as you get closer you'll realise that it is only this shape from the front, as smooth slopes lead gently to the summit from every other direction. Nevertheless this fell has been coined the Matterhorn of Easedale, after the great conical mountain in the Swiss Alps.

Blea Rigg marks the divide between Easedale and Langdale and from here you can climb north-west for Sergeant Man, a rocky knob with good views down Easedale. A fainter path continues onto High Raise, which is generally regarded as the centre of Lakeland and as you'd expect the views from the summit fill all 360 degrees of the compass. It's worth taking the time to take in this view, as there is no path for the next short section. In particular, the way ahead towards Scafell Pike can be easily identified.

You need to cross open unpathed fell to Stake Pass at the head of the Langdale valley and then walk around the back of Rossett Pike to Angle Tarn. Here you join the ancient trade route between Borrowdale and Langdale which leads easily to Esk Hause. Scafell Pike is close and easily reached from Esk Hause, but an easier, shorter and more direct route to Ravenglass can be enjoyed by descending into Upper Eskdale. A clear path takes you under the cliffs of Esk Pike, Ill Crag, Scafell Pike and Scafell to the Great Moss. The path leads out of the valley to Brotherilkeld Farm at the base of Hardknott Pass in the Eskdale valley. You could shorten the day here by taking an overnight stop at the Eskdale Youth Hostel or the Woolpack Inn. You could even catch the Ravenglass and Eskdale Railway. But if you are still strong in the leg, use the paths that trace the River Esk as far as Eskdale Green. You can then climb over Muncaster Fell and descend Fell Lane to the A595 from where a short road walk takes you into Ravenglass.

SILECROFT TO BORROWDALE VIA ESKDAKE

Black Combe rises like a great whaleback from the level surroundings of the Whicham valley, overlooking the far south-western seaboard of the Lake District. It marks the toe of a long mountain ridge that stretches to Eskdale, a ridge that is wild, remote and rarely walked. The ridge is also home to Devoke Water, Lakeland's highest tarn, where fine views to the Scafell massif are on show to those few who make the effort to visit the lake shore in this quiet backwater.

This walk exposes two very different aspects of Lakeland's character: after a traverse of the Black Combe ridge and a descent into Eskdale, the tone of the walk changes from the wild, barren moors to the towering cliffs and rocky paths of the Scafell range.

DAY ONE

There is a railway station at Silecroft not far from Millom and this provides the ideal start to the walk for those using public transport. A road takes you to Whicham church from where a path leads to Kirkbank and a clear green swathe which leads you onto the back of Black Combe. The broad and well-made cart track must have been used as a trade route or to serve the copper mining activity that took place under White Combe. Today the mines are quiet, but the path allows easy access to the summit plateau from where the most outstanding views reveal themselves. On a clear day you can sit back to enjoy the twinkling sea and the hazy outlines of the Isle of Man, Snowdonia, Ireland and Scotland. Then there's the coastal scene from St Bees to the Isle of Walney

WALK FACTS

Start	Silecroft, GR 130820
Finish	Seatoller, GR 245138
Distance	Day one: 24km (15 miles)
	Day two: 16km (10 miles)
Total ascent	Day one: 1090m (3576ft)
	Day two: 1400m (4593ft)
Time	Day one: 8 hours
	Day two: 8 hours

Difficulty A long, high-level walk across wild, open fells with few paths where good navigational skills will be required. The second day climbs over Scafell Pike the highest mountain in England, with clear rocky paths

Accommodation Youth hostels, campsites and B&Bs at Eskdale and Seatoller in Borrowdale. B&Bs and campsites near Silecroft and Millom

Public transport Railway services link Millom and Silecroft to the west coast main line. Bus services from Seatoller have connections with the main line railway station at Penrith

to enjoy, but most impressive of all is the inland mountain panorama that extends to the distant hazy outline of the Pennines, the high moorland spine of England.

The route follows the long broad ridge of Black Combe north-east to Stroupdale Head and then follows a north-north-west direction over Swinside Fell to Stoneside Hill. A short walk from here leads to a road that crosses the fell to allow easy access to the tops for those with weary legs. Buck Barrow comes next, providing fine retrospective views to Black Combe and then you arrive at Whitfell with its trig point, cairn and stone wind-break. Cross Stainton Fell to the rocky crown of Yoadcastle. This is shortly followed by the cairned top of Woodend Height, with its views of Devoke Water and the wild moor of Birker Fell leading into the lush valley of Eskdale, with the great bulk of the Scafell massif dominating the skyline beyond.

A track takes you from Devoke Water over the Ulpha Pass road and down to High Ground and Birkerthwaite. You can then pick your way through the fields to Stanley Force, a fine waterfall that tumbles over a rocky lip at the head of a narrow ravine.

147

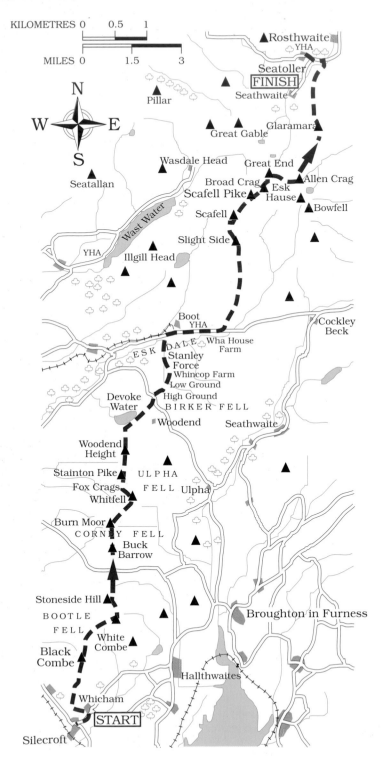

KILOMETRES 0   0.5   1

MILES 0   1.5   3

ALONG THE WAY

Devoke Water is the highest tarn in the Lake District. The name means 'the dark one' which no doubt is partly a reference to the wild, bleak and desolate surroundings that the tarn occupies. Originally these wild moors were covered in forest until being cleared by Neolithic people to provide grazing land for sheep. Many prehistoric remains have been discovered in the area including evidence of burial grounds, stone circles, settlements and field systems.

St Catherine's Church stands on a bank of the River Esk in Eskdale. It was built of local granite in the seventeenth century and has a striking memorial in the graveyard to Thomas Dobson, who died in 1910 aged eighty-three. 'Tommy' as he was known was a popular fellow who was the master of the Eskdale and Ennerdale foxhounds.

Scafell's northern cliffs are famous throughout Britain for their outstanding rock climbing and today they attract rock gymnasts throughout the year as they have done since the pioneers first started to discover the sport in the late nineteenth century. But the western slopes of Scafell are like another mountain when compared to those towering cliffs to the north. On the west, Scafell descends in one huge grassy slope, devoid of rock, crag and gully. But this does not detract from the appeal, as what these slopes lack in airy delights they more than make up for in their views which can extend on a clear day to Snowdonia, the Isle of Man and the Solway Firth.

Opposite: Looking towards Glaramara with Esk Hause cairn in the foreground

The scene is a spectacular one, with the roar of the crashing water, the spray filling the air and beams of sunlight breaking through the canopy of trees. A walk along the banks of the River Esk will lead you to a choice of accommodation in Eskdale.

DAY TWO

It's time to climb a mountain and step from wild, lonely moors onto well-trodden rocky trails. There are many ways to climb Scafell from Eskdale and one path leaves the road opposite Wha House Farm. The clear track takes you steadily onto the shoulder of Slight Side. The climb is long, but with extensive views to the rear over Eskdale and east into Upper Eskdale, there are plenty of reasons to stop and take a breather.

Slight Side marks your arrival on the final approach to Scafell's summit. Here the angle eases and the cliffs to your right begin to grow, until finally there is no easy escape and you arrive at the summit surrounded with steep slopes and cliffs. From the top you can well understand how it was originally thought that Scafell was the highest point, while the neighbouring summit of Scafell Pike was described as merely 'the pikes near Scafell'. Today we know different and it's Scafell Pike at

Early morning on Glaramara with the Langdale Pikes in the distance

977m (3205ft) which holds the title of the highest point in England. But Scafell too is a great mountain at 964m (3163ft) and for climbers it is the finest mountain in England as its cliffs provide many fine and testing routes. It is also these cliffs that bar a direct passage between Scafell and Scafell Pike. The walker's route is known as the Foxes Tarn Path and this leaves the summit of Scafell in an easterly direction to descend steeply past a tiny tarn, emerging below the cliffs to the east of Mickledore. You then have to scramble up the scree to Mickledore and the nearby summit of Scafell Pike. Once again Scafell dominates the view and those massive cliffs are clearly the highlight of the whole mountain massif.

To end your day in Borrowdale there are a variety of routes that can be followed from Scafell Pike, but in an attempt to stay high, I favour the traverse of Broad Crag and Ill Crag to Esk Hause. But don't forget Great End along the way for its view to Borrowdale is wonderful. A walk over Glaramara from Esk Hause brings views of Great End's mighty northern cliffs and then it's downhill all the way to Borrowdale.

CONISTON TO KESWICK VIA WASDALE

A rugged mountain crest extends through the heart of the Lake District making it possible to walk from one side of the National Park to the other without leaving the wild mountain tops. This walk manages to capture all the finest fells and the loftiest summits of the greatest ranges in the Lake District, taking in as it does the Coniston Fells, Langdale Fells, Scafell massif, Great Gable, Dale Head and finally the ridge that descends to Cat Bells. Along the way you visit Wasdale Head, where the exploration of the Lakeland fells stepped up a gear in the nineteenth century. The last fell on the walk, Cat Bells, is for many their first step into Lakeland fell walking. This walk is perhaps the greatest mountain traverse of the Lake District.

DAY ONE

The small village of Coniston can easily be reached by public transport making it the ideal start for a mountain traverse of the Lake District. The Old Man of Coniston towers over the village and this is your first objective. The Sun Hotel near the centre of Coniston is a popular hikers' haunt and a path beside the building leads into the Coppermines valley. This is a popular route onto the tops, making it difficult to get lost. You climb steadily through the disused mine workings where rusting iron mixes with tumbledown stone buildings and dark mine shafts. Climbing higher you rise above the turquoise waters of Low Water, whose colouring has been tinted by the rich copper deposits of the area. Still higher the whole Coppermines valley opens out beneath you, with the fells twisting and rising to the great bulk of Wetherlam.

WALK FACTS

Start	Coniston, GR 305976
Finish	Keswick, GR 265235
Distance	Day one: 24km (15 miles)
	Day two: 19.3km (12 miles)
Total ascent	Day one: 1800m (5905ft)
	Day two: 1300m (4265ft)
Time	Day one: 12 hours
	Day two: 7 hours

Difficulty A very long route over the highest fells of the Lake District with a large amount of ascent. There are clear paths throughout and many alternative escape routes that could be used in foul weather

Accommodation Youth hostels, B&Bs, hotels and campsites at Coniston, Wasdale and Keswick

Public transport Regular bus services link Coniston and Keswick to the railway stations at Windermere and Penrith. There is no public transport in Wasdale. A regular bus service also extends down Borrowdale to Seatoller and down Langdale, which may be useful in an emergency

Finally the summit of the Old Man of Coniston comes underfoot and you are rewarded with a view that extends into the heart of the Lake District and beyond. This mighty traverse takes in much of the mountain scenery ahead but begins by completing a ridge walk around the Coniston range of fells to Swirl How. This is a tremendous walk along a broad ridge that is narrow enough to provide fine views on both sides, while being wide enough to make it easy.

You leave the Coniston fells by descending to Wrynose Pass and then stepping onto the Langdale Fells. A path takes you to Red Tarn from where you can climb onto the back of Crinkle Crags, with their views to Langdale and the mighty Scafell massif. Bowfell comes underfoot soon and again it is Langdale and Scafell that hold the most attention. Esk Pike is traversed on the way to Esk Hause and then you begin the walk over the highest land in England. The path onto Scafell Pike is well marked but the plateau is so large that it's worth wandering off route a little to visit Great End, Broad Crag and Loft Crag, for the views from these summits are far superior to those of Scafell Pike. But Scafell Pike is

The southern end of Crinkle Crags in the Langdale valley with Bowfell on the right

Opposite: Skiddaw rises above Derwent Water and Keswick from Cat Bells

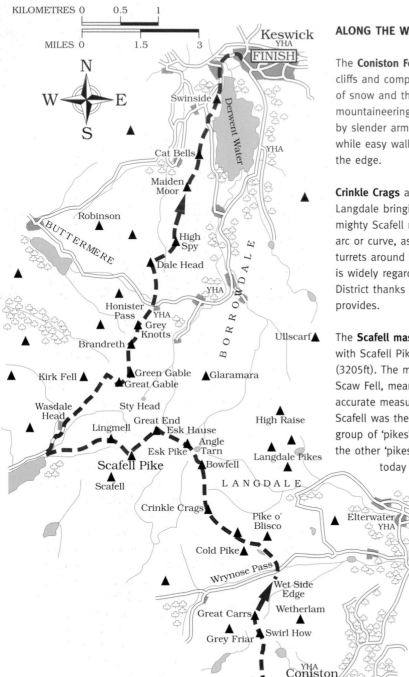

KILOMETRES 0   0.5   1

MILES 0   1.5   3

Keswick
YHA
FINISH

Swinside

Derwent Water

YHA

Cat Bells

Maiden Moor

Robinson

BUTTERMERE

High Spy

Dale Head

YHA

Honister Pass

YHA

Grey Knotts

Brandreth

BORROWDALE

Ullscarf

Kirk Fell

Green Gable

Great Gable

Glaramara

Wasdale Head

Sty Head

Great End

Lingmell

Esk Hause

Angle Tarn

High Raise

Esk Pike

Langdale Pikes

Scafell Pike

Bowfell

Scafell

LANGDALE

Crinkle Crags

Pike o' Blisco

Elterwater
YHA

Cold Pike

Wrynose Pass

Wet Side Edge

Great Carrs

Wetherlam

Grey Friar

Swirl How

YHA
Coniston
YHA
START

Dow Crag

Old Man of Coniston

ALONG THE WAY

The **Coniston Fells** are rough and rocky with towering cliffs and complex contours at every turn. Add a dusting of snow and they are transformed into fine mountaineering country. The range of summits is linked by slender arms that bring airy views over the cliffs while easy walking is maintained if you steer clear of the edge.

Crinkle Crags and **Bowfell** rise around the head of Langdale bringing views to both Langdale and the mighty Scafell massif. The name Crinkle Crags means arc or curve, as this is the shape of this range of rocky turrets around the head of the Langdale valley. Bowfell is widely regarded as the finest viewpoint in the Lake District thanks to the extensive panorama that it provides.

The **Scafell massif** marks the highest land in England with Scafell Pike claiming the highest point at 977m (3205ft). The mountain range was originally known as Scaw Fell, meaning 'Fell of the Rocky Tops' and before accurate measurements were made it was thought that Scafell was the higher while Scafell Pike was merely a group of 'pikes' or summits overshadowed by Scafell, the other 'pikes' being Ill Crag and Broad Crag. But today it is Scafell Pike that has no peer, while neighbouring Scafell is rarely visited except by rock climbers who travel from all over Britain to do battle with its towering northern cliffs.

the highest point and you'll no doubt celebrate your achievement more here than when visiting those neighbouring viewpoints.

Your overnight rest is at Wasdale Head and the best descent is via Lingmell as it provides a fine view to Scafell's towering northern cliffs.

DAY TWO

The sanctuary of Wasdale Head has the mountains and the mood that capture the spirit of exploring the Lakeland fells. It was here that the great mountaineering pioneers gathered during the last century in their tweeds and hobnailed boots. Today little has changed: there is still only a small cluster of buildings, including an inn, an outdoor shop, a campsite and a scattering of farms. Great Gable seems to plug the head of the valley, with its tantalising jumble of rock just below the summit drawing walkers and climbers onto its slopes today just as it did when the pioneers first did battle with these mountains.

The way to Keswick begins by climbing Great Gable. There are numerous routes to the top but the most logical is to follow the walled lane past the tiny St Olaf church to the last farm. A path then traces the foot of the fells and crosses Gable Beck. Here you can climb steeply up between the slopes of Kirk Fell and Great Gable to Beck Head from where Great Gable's

summit is within easy reach over a rocky path.

The pyramidal shape of Great Gable allows outstanding views from the top, but you have to walk down the southern slopes to Westmorland Cairn to get the finest views that extend from Wasdale Head across Wast Water to the coast. Turning your back on the view, you'll find paths leading to Green Gable, with views down the length of Ennerdale. Then you steadily descend over Brandreth and Grey Knotts to Honister Pass. To end the walk, step onto the Newlands Fells by clambering quite steeply alongside a fence to Dale Head. This is a refreshing summit after the dim confines of Honister Pass. The view extends down the length of the Newlands valley to distant Skiddaw. The end is now in your sights and it's almost all downhill! So walk steeply at first down to Dalehead Tarn from where a wonderful rolling ridge walk sweeps above Borrowdale and Derwent Water to Cat Bells. Many youngsters have been introduced to fell walking by way of Cat Bells. With views that include Skiddaw, Blencathra, Grisedale Pike, Causey Pike, Borrowdale, Derwent Water, Keswick and Bassenthwaite Lake, it is surely the finest introduction to walking there is in the Lake District, while this long and tough mountain traverse from Coniston to Keswick is surely one of the Lake District's greatest backpacking adventures.

Opposite: View towards Windermere from Loughrigg Fell above Ambleside

GETTING ABOUT

Rail Services

General train services:
Tel: (0345) 484950
Ravenglass and Eskdale Railway:
Tel: (01229) 717171

Bus Services
Stagecoach Cumberland:
Tel: (01946) 63222
Mountain Goat:
Tel: (017687) 73962

Lake Cruises
Derwent Water
Keswick Launch Company:
Tel: (017687) 72263
Windermere
Bowness Bay Boating Company:
Tel: (015394) 43360
Windermere Iron Steamboat
Company:
Tel: (015395) 31188
Coniston
Coniston Launch:
Tel: (015394) 36216
Steam Yacht Gondola:
Tel: (015394) 41288

Ullswater
Ullswater Motor Yachts:
Tel: (017684) 82229

National Park Visitor Centre
Brockhole:
Tel: (015394) 46601

Lake District National Park Weather Line
Keswick: *Tel:* (017687) 75757

Tourist Information Centres
Ambleside:
Tel: (015394) 32582
Barrow in Furness:
Tel: (01229) 870156
Borrowdale:
Tel: (017687) 77294
Bowness on Windermere:
Tel: (015394) 42895
Cockermouth:
Tel: (01900) 822634
Coniston:
Tel: (015394) 41533
Egremont:
Tel: (01946) 820693

Glenridding:
Tel: (017684) 82414
Grange over Sands:
Tel: (015395) 34026
Grasmere:
Tel: (015394) 35245
Hawkshead:
Tel: (015394) 36525
Kendal:
Tel: (015395) 725758
Keswick:
Tel: (017687) 72645
Penrith:
Tel: (01768) 867466
Pooley Bridge:
Tel: (017684) 86530
Seascale:
Tel: (019467) 76510
Waterhead (Ambleside):
Tel: (015394) 32729
Whitehaven:
Tel: (01946) 852939
Windermere:
Tel: (015394) 46499
Workington:
Tel: (01900) 602923

ACKNOWLEDGEMENTS

This book could not have been produced without the help and support of many people. It draws on many guidebooks and reference works that are already published. In particular Alfred Wainwright charted routes across virtually the whole of the Lake District and his guidebooks were of considerable use while compiling this book.

Once again Jeremy Ashcroft has been particularly helpful with the design and drawing of the maps – they would not have been so good without his assistance.

Thanks also to all those walkers who have wandered the fells with me in search of that perfect photo opportunity, including Ian Winchester, David Winchester, Alan Wright, Andrew Haigh, Steve Robinson, Pete Savin, Julian Thomas, Guy Harrop, John Newsome and Tim Butcher. Thanks also to Dawn Gibson and Nima, my most constant companions on the fells.

Finally, my thanks to those who I unintentionally failed to acknowledge.

BIBLIOGRAPHY

Allen, B., *On High Lakeland Fells* (Pic Publications, 1988)

Ashcroft, J., *Britain's Highest Peaks* (David & Charles, 1993)

Birkett, B., *Complete Lakeland Fells* (Collins Willow, 1994)

Collingwood, W. G., *The Lake Counties* (J. M. Dent & Sons, 1942)

Fraser, M., *Companion to Lakeland* (Methuen & Co, 1948)

Griffin, A. H., *In Mountain Lakeland* (Guardian Press, 1969)

Griffin, A. H., *Adventuring in Lakeland* (Robert Hale, 1980)

Hankinson, A., *The First Tigers* (Melbecks Books, 1984)

Hankinson, A., *A Century on the Crags* (J.M. Dent & Sons Ltd, 1988)

Hindle, B. P., *Roads and Trackways of the Lake District* (Moorland Publishing, 1984)

Lindop, G., *A Literary Guide to the Lake District* (Chatto & Windus, 1993)

Marsh, T., *The Lake Mountains Volumes 1 & 2* (Hodder & Stoughton, 1987)

Nicholson, N., *Cumberland and Westmorland* (Robert Hale, 1949)

Nicholson, N., *Portrait of the Lakes* (Robert Hale, 1980)

Nicholson, N., *Norman Nicholson's Lakeland* (Robert Hale, 1991)

Unsworth, W., *The High Fells of Lakeland* (Cicerone, 1992)

Wainwright, A., *A Pictorial Guide to the Lakeland Fells* (7 volumes) (Michael Joseph, 1955 onwards)

Welsh, F., *Companion Guide to the Lake District* (Collins, 1989)

157

INDEX

Aire Force 110, 111
Allen Crags 62
Allerdale Ramble 17,18
Ambleside 8, 74, 83, 84, 95–7, 99, 106, 118–20, 124, 134, 136–8
Angle Tarn 73, 90, 97, 98, 145, 146
Angletarn Pikes 98
Arnsbarrow Hill 122
Arnside 78
Arthur's Pike 107
Askham 141
Atkinson, John 47

Bakestall 16, 35
Bampton 104, 105, 106, 141
Band, The 75
Bannerdale 98
Bannisdale 102
Barton Fell 134
Bassenthwaite 17, 18, 19, 35, 36, 86
Bassenthwaite Lake 18, 30, 35, 36, 37, 155
Beacon Tarn 121, 128
Beck Head 40, 46, 61
Bell, Rev John 96
Belles Island 119
Bethecar Moor 122
Binsey 17, 18
Birker Fell 147
Birkhouse Moor 94
Blackbeck Tarn 20
Black Combe 48, 51, 130, 147
Black Crag 24
Black Sail 40, 45, 46, 47, 61
Blake Fell 24
Bleaberry Fell 71, 85, 87
Bleaberry Tarn 20
Blea Rigg 88, 146
Blease Fell 14
Blea Tarn 44, 51, 79, 87
Blelham Tarn 120
Blencathra 14, 16, 24, 26, 30, 34, 71, 112, 155
Blengdale 50
Brack Barrow 56
Braithwaite 35, 37
Branstree 104
Brantwood 122, 123
Brigsteer 117

Brunt Fell 103
Boat How 50
Boathow Crag 46
Bonscale Pike 107
Border End 62, 75
Boredale Hause 97, 98, 111, 145
Borrowdale 27, 30, 57, 60–2, 64, 65, 73, 85–7, 147, 150, 155
Bowfell 26, 34, 52, 54, 56, 62, 63, 73–5, 79, 88, 89, 130, 143, 151, 154
Bowness 118, 119, 124, 133
Bowness Knott 45, 47
Bowscale Fell 14
Bowscale Tarn 14
Bridge End 110
Broad Crag 57, 66, 75, 150, 151
Broad Stand 63, 65
Broom Fell 34, 35, 37
Brotherswater 98
Brougham 95
Brown Haw 56
Brown Hill 100, 111
Brown Pike 84, 130
Brown Rigg 54
Broughton in Furness 54–6, 127, 129, 130
Broughton Mills 130
Buck Barrow 147
Buckholme Island 18
Burnbank Fell 24
Burnbanks 99, 104
Burnmoor Tarn 40, 42, 43, 44, 61
Buttermere 8, 19, 20, 21, 24, 25, 26, 27, 31, 32, 34, 45, 85

Caldbeck 17, 18
Calfhow Pike 112
Campbell, Donald 123
Carrock Fell 14
Carron Crag 122, 132, 133
Carter Ground 56
Cartmell Fell 117
Castle How 17
Castle Rock of Triermain 113, 114
Cat Bells 27, 30, 31, 85, 86, 151, 155
Catstycam 72
Caudale Moor 95, 96, 124
Causey Pike 27, 30, 31, 155

Caw 54, 56, 130
Claife Heights 120
Clough Head 112
Coast to Coast Walk 91, 98, 99, 102, 140, 145, 146
Cockermouth 17, 18, 32, 33, 34
Cofa Pike 97
Coledale Hause 26 , 34
Coleridge, Samuel Taylor 47, 63
Colwith Force 137
Coniston 76, 78, 79, 81, 82, 84, 88, 121, 127, 128, 151, 154, 155
Coniston Water 82, 121, 122, 123, 131, 133
Coomb Height 16
Corridor Route 40, 65
Crag Fell 46
Crag Hill 26, 27, 30, 31
Crinkle Crags 52, 62, 73, 74, 88, 90, 143, 151, 154
Crook Crag 52, 54, 55
Crosthwaite 117
Crummock Water 20, 21, 24, 25, 26, 31, 34
Cumbria Way 16, 17, 76, 78, 121, 128, 137
Cunswick Scar 116

Dale End 90
Dalegarth 42
Dale Head 19, 27, 85, 87, 151, 155
Dales Way 116
Darling How 37
Deepdale Hause 93, 97
Derwent Water 14, 19, 27, 30, 35, 64, 65, 85, 86, 87, 155
Devoke Water 52, 53, 147, 148
Dixon Memorial 94
Dobson, Tommy 148
Dockray 111
Doctor's Bridge 56, 84
Dollywagon Pike 67, 71, 72, 93, 94, 97
Dow Crag 76, 79, 84, 121, 127, 128, 130
Dubs Quarry 19, 20, 21
Dunmail Raise 15, 70
Dunnerdale 128, 130

Easedale 67, 71, 146
Eel Tarn 42
Egremont, Lord 18
Elterwater 73, 77, 78, 88, 90
Ennerdale 20, 40, 45, 46, 47, 48, 50, 61, 155
Ennerdale Water 46, 48
Eskdale 42–4, 51–5, 62, 64, 66, 73, 74, 75, 81, 84, 88, 128, 134, 136, 137, 142, 146–8, 150
Esk Hause 57, 60, 62, 64, 66, 73, 74, 86, 146, 150, 151
Esk Pike 62, 73, 75, 143, 146, 151
Esthwaite Water 133

Fairfield 71, 91, 93, 95, 97,98, 145
Falcon Crag 87
Fellbarrow 26, 32
Fleetwith Pike 19, 20, 27, 87
Force Mills 126, 131
Foule Crags 14
Foxes Tarn 40, 42, 61, 64, 66, 75, 150
Fox Haw 130
Froswick 124, 134, 138
Furness Abbey 53
Furness Railway 82, 127

Garburn Pass 138
Gasgale Crags 26
Gatesgarth Pass 100, 104, 138
Gavel Fell 24
Gillercombe 61
Gillerthwaite 34, 47, 48
Gimmer Crag 73, 88
Glaramara 57, 62, 64, 86, 87, 150
Glencoyne 111
Glenderaterra Beck 14
Glenridding 70, 91, 93, 95, 98, 107, 110, 111, 112
Goat's Hause 79, 84
Gough Memorial 91, 94
Gowbarrow Fell 111
Graham, Bob 66
Grange 60, 65
Grasmere 65, 66, 67, 68, 70, 71, 72, 88, 91, 93, 94, 96, 142, 143, 145
Grasmoor 24, 26, 32, 34, 143, 145

Graystones 34
Great Borne 45
Great Calva 15, 16
Great Dodd 112
Great End 57, 64, 65, 66, 73, 150, 151
Great Gable 19, 20, 21, 26, 27, 34, 38, 40–2, 45, 46, 48, 57, 60, 61, 62, 86, 87, 151, 155
Great Knott 90
Great Ladstones 100
Great Lingy Fell 16
Great Moss 74, 75, 146
Great Meldrum 111
Great Mell Fell 111
Great Rigg 97
Great Stickle 54, 130
Great Tongue 93, 94
Great Worm Crag 52, 54
Greenburn 79, 83
Green Crag 20, 51, 52, 54
Green Gable 61, 155
Greenhead 17
Green How 18, 40
Greenside 112
Greenup Edge 67, 71
Greta Gill 40
Grey Friar 83
Grisedale 71, 72, 91, 93, 94, 95, 112, 143, 145
Grisedale Pike 30, 35, 36, 37, 155
Grisedale Tarn 67, 72, 93, 94, 97, 143, 145
Grizedale Forest 118, 120, 122, 124, 125, 126, 131, 133
Gummer's How 117, 120

Hallin Fell 107
Hardknott Pass 51, 62, 63, 64, 74, 75, 83, 84, 136, 137, 146
Harper Hill 104
Harrison Stickle 88
Hart Crag 97
Harter Fell 51, 56, 83, 100, 104, 138
Hart Side 111
Hartsop 100
Haweswater 98, 99, 100, 104, 105, 106, 134, 138, 141–3, 145
Hawkshead 121, 124, 126, 131, 132, 133
Haycock 38, 40, 46, 48
Hayeswater 100, 138
Hay Stacks 21, 45

Helm Crag 71
Helvellyn 15, 65, 67, 72, 85, 87, 91, 93, 94, 95, 96, 97, 112, 114, 142, 145
Heron Pike 97, 111
Hesket Newmarket 33
Heughscar Hill 134 High Crag 20, 45
High Dewaldeth 18
High Dodd 111
High Ireby 18
High Lorton 32, 33, 37
High Pike 15, 16, 97
High Raise 66, 99, 142, 146
High Rigg 113, 114
High Seat 85
High Snockrigg 31
High Spy 27, 85
High Stile 19, 20, 26, 31, 34, 45, 46
High Street 95, 96, 98, 100, 104, 106, 107, 111, 124, 134, 138, 142, 143, 145
High Tongue 84
High Tove 71, 87
High Wray 120
Hindscarth 19, 27, 31
Hinkler Memorial 96
Hobcarton Crags 37
Honister 19, 27, 85, 86, 155
Hope, Augustus 25
Hopegill Head 26, 34, 35, 36, 37
Howtown 107

Ill Bell 124, 134, 138
Ill Crag 57, 66, 75, 146, 150
Illgill Head 40, 44
Innominate Tarn 20, 45

Jack's Rake 89
Jenkin Hill 35, 67
Jenkin's Crag 137

Kendal 33, 115, 116, 117
Kentmere 101, 102, 104
Kepple Cove 72
Keswick 14, 16, 30, 31, 33, 35, 65, 66, 67, 68, 70, 112, 114, 134, 151, 155
Kidsty Pike 99, 143, 145
Kiln Bank Cross 130
Kirk Fell 34, 40, 46, 48, 61
Kirkstone Pass 95

Knowe Crags 14
Ladyside Pike 36, 37
Lakeside 124, 120
Langdale 62, 73, 75, 76, 78, 79, 88, 89, 90, 151
Langdale Pikes 73, 120, 124, 146
Lang How 88
Langhowe Pike 103
Langstrath 62
Lank Rigg 48, 50
Lanty's Tarn 112
Latrigg 14, 16, 35, 67
Latterbarrow 120, 124
Legburthwaite 67, 72
Leonard, Arthur 27
Leven Estuary 117
Levers Water 79
Ling Fell 35, 37
Lingmell 40, 42, 44, 65
Lingmoor Fell 88, 90
Little Calva 16
Little Fell 78
Little Langdale 79, 83, 137
Little Man 35, 67
Little Meldrum 111
Loadpot Hill 99, 106, 107, 134
Loft Crag 88, 151
Longlands 17
Longsleddale 100, 101, 103, 138
Longthwaite 85
Lonscale Fell 35
Lord's Seat 34, 35, 37
Lord's Rake 65
Lorton Vale 26, 32, 33, 34
Lower Man 67, 72, 114
Loweswater 24, 25, 26, 31, 33, 34
Low Fell 26, 34, 103
Lowick 121
Low Kop 99, 106
Low Pike 97
Low Rigg 113, 114
Low Water 79, 84, 151
Lucock, Joshua 33
Lyth Valley 115, 116, 117

Maiden Moor 27, 85
Mardale 96, 98, 104, 104, 105, 106, 145
Mardale Ill Bell 100, 106, 138
Martindale 107
Maryport 18
Mellbreak 24, 34
Mickleden 73, 90
Mickledore 40, 42, 61, 63, 64, 65,

75, 150
Middle Crag 71, 87
Middle Fell 38, 40, 48
Miterdale 42, 44
Moor Howe 117, 118, 138
Moot Hall 65, 66
Mosedale 14, 61, 100, 103, 138
Moss Eccles Tarn 120, 124
Mosser Fell 26
Muncaster Fell 51–3, 137, 146

Naddle Valley 113
Nan Bield Pass 100, 104, 106, 138
Napes Needle 60
Near Sawrey 120, 124
Nethermost Cove 72, 96
Nethermost Pike 72, 93, 94, 97
Newby Bridge 115, 117, 118, 119, 120, 124, 126
Newlands 19, 27, 30, 31, 85

Old Dungeon Ghyll Hotel 73, 75, 78, 88
Old Man of Coniston 76, 78, 79, 83, 84, 121, 127, 128, 130, 151
Ore Gap 62, 63, 75, 90
Orrest Head 118, 119, 138
Outhwaite 17
Otley, Jonathan 47
Over Water 17

Papcastle 33
Parr, Catherine 116
Patterdale 91, 93, 95–8, 100, 111, 145
Pavey Ark 88, 89
Peel Island 123
Peel, John 18
Penrith 8, 18, 33, 99, 106, 134, 136, 138, 141, 145
Pier's Gill 40, 65
Piked Howe 101
Pike o' Blisco 76, 79, 88, 90
Pike o' Stickle 88
Pillar 20, 21, 27, 38, 40, 41, 45, 46, 47, 48, 130
Place Fell 111
Pooley Bridge 107, 110, 111, 141
Portinscale 27, 85
Potter, Beatrix 124, 126, 132
Pottergill 26
Potter Tarn 101

Raise 67, 72, 114
Rankin, Sir Robert 129
Ransome, Arthur 123
Raven Crag 73, 114, 130
Ravenglass 8, 42, 44, 51, 52, 53, 54, 55, 74, 81, 134, 136, 137, 142, 146
Raven's Barrow 117
Rawlinson Nab 120, 124
Rawsley, Canon 49
Red Pike 19, 20, 45
Red Screes 95, 124
Red Tarn 79, 90, 96, 114, 151
Richardson, John 113
Riggindale 106, 143, 145
Ritson, Will 43, 60
River Bleng 50
River Brathay 78
River Caldew 14
River Cocker 18, 32
River Crake 121
River Derwent 17, 18, 27, 65, 85, 86
River Duddon 54, 84, 137
River Eamont 134, 136
River Esk 44, 51, 62, 74, 75, 84, 137, 148, 150
River Glenderamarkin 14
River Greta 67
River Kent 101
River Leven 120
River Lickle 54, 130
River Lowther 141, 145
River Mite 44
River Sprint 103
River Winster 116, 117
Robin Hood's Bay 91, 102
Robinson's Cairn 46, 47
Roehead 107
Rosthwaite 87
Round How 40
Rowling End 31
Ruskin, John 123
Rusland 131
Ruthwaite 18
Rydal 68

Sadgill 103
Sail 31
Sale Fell 35, 37
Santon Bridge 43
Satterthwaite 126, 131, 133
Sawrey, John Gilpin 129
Scafell 24, 38, 40–2, 44, 48, 51,

52, 54, 56, 57, 61–7, 73–5, 84, 130, 143, 146–8, 150, 151, 154
Scafell Pike 6, 26, 34, 38, 40–4, 48, 57, 62–7, 74, 75, 84, 87, 130, 142, 143, 146, 150, 151, 154
Scalderskew 50
Scale Force 20, 21
Scale Knott 26, 34
Scales Tarn 14
Scarth Gap 20, 45, 47
School Knott 118
Scoat Fell 40, 46, 48
Scout Scar 115, 116, 117
Scot Rake 134
Scott, Sir Walter 113
Seatallan 38, 40, 48
Seathwaite 60, 61, 64, 65, 87
Seatoller 57, 61, 62, 64, 65, 85, 87
Selside Pike 104
Sergeant Man 88, 146
Shap 98, 99, 101, 102, 103, 104, 138, 140–3
Sharp Edge 14, 15
Sheffield Pike 111
Side Pike 90
Silver How 88
Siney Tarn 44, 51
Skeggles Water 103
Skelgill 31
Skelwith Bridge 78, 137
Skiddaw 14–19, 24, 26, 27, 30, 34, 35, 36, 37, 64, 65, 66, 67, 71, 85, 155
Sleddale 98, 100
Sleet Fell 111
Small Water 103, 106, 138
Smithy Fell 26, 32
Sourfoot Fell 26, 32, 34
Sourmilk Gill 61, 146
Spark Bridge 121, 122, 131, 132, 133
Sprinkling Tarn 64
St Bees Head 91, 102, 147
St John's in the Vale 15, 71, 112, 113, 114
St Sunday Crag 72, 91, 93, 94, 97, 145
Stake Pass 66, 88, 146
Starling Dodd 45
Standing Crag 71
Stanley Gill 137, 147
Staveley 101, 102, 103

Staveley-in-Cartmel 117
Steeple 40, 46, 48
Sticks Pass 67, 70, 72, 112, 114
Stickle Pike 54, 130
Stickle Tarn 88, 130
Stonethwaite 85
Stony Cove Pike 95, 97
Stony Tarn 42
Stott Park Bobbin Mill 124, 125
Striding Edge 15, 72, 91, 94, 95, 96, 97, 112, 114, 145
Stybarrow Dodd 112
Sty Head 40, 62, 64, 65
Sulurian Way 133
Swindale 98, 103, 104, 138
Swineside Knott 111
Swinside 34, 147
Swirl How 76, 79, 127, 151
Swirrel Edge 114

Tailbert 103
Tarn Crags 14, 52
Tarn Hows 76, 77, 78
Tennyson, Alfred 123
Thackthwaite 32
Thirlmere 15, 67, 68, 71, 72, 85, 87, 114
Thorneythwaite Fell 57, 62
Thornthwaite Crag 95, 100, 134, 138
Three Shires Stone 79
Three Tarns 62
Threlkeld 112, 114
Thresthwaite Mouth 95, 100
Thunacar Knott 88
Tilberthwaite 83, 121
Tom Heights 78
Tongue How 50
Tongue Moor 44
Top o' Selside 122, 133
Troutbeck 118 , 124, 137, 138

Uldale Fell 17
Ullscarf 71
Ullswater 91, 93, 107, 110, 111, 142, 145
Ulpha 54, 147
Ulverston 78
Underbarrow 116

Waingap 116
Wainwright, Alfred 15, 20, 21, 30, 45, 71, 89, 91, 129, 140, 146

Wallace, William 52
Walla Crag 71, 87
Walna Scar 55, 56, 79, 84, 128, 130
Wandope 26, 31, 34
Wansfell Pike 118, 138
Wasdale 38, 40, 41, 42, 43, 44, 46, 47, 48, 51, 57, 60, 61, 73, 88, 151,155
Wast Water 6, 40, 43, 44, 48, 61, 155
Watendlath 85, 87
Watermillock 111
Watson's Dodd 112
Westmorland Cairn 41, 61, 155
Westray 34
Wether Hill 106
Wetherlam 77, 78, 79, 83, 90, 121, 127, 151
Wet Sleddale 103, 141
Whinlatter 32, 33, 34, 36, 37
Whin Rigg 40, 44
Whitbarrow 115, 116, 117
White Combe 147
Whiteless Pike 26, 31, 34
White Pike 54, 56, 130
White Side 67, 72
Whiteside 26
Whiteside Bank 114
Whiteside Pike 101, 102
Whitewater Dash 16, 35
Whitfell 147
Whoap 50
Wilberforce, William 66
Windermere 6, 15, 33, 68, 83, 95, 96, 115, 117–20, 124, 131, 133, 134, 137, 138, 141
Windy Gap 45, 61
Winster 115, 116, 117
Wise Een Tarn 120, 124
Woodend Height 147
Woolpack Inn 51, 52, 56, 84, 146
Wordsworth, William 18, 21, 32, 33, 47, 55, 89, 91, 110, 119, 126, 132, 143, 146
Wrynose Pass 56, 79, 83, 134, 151
Wythburn 71
Wythop 37

Yewdale Beck 78, 121, 122
Yoke 134, 138